LEADERSHIP FABLES BY PATRICK LENCIONI

The Five Temptations of a CEO

▲

The Four Obsessions of an Extraordinary Executive

▲

The Five Dysfunctions of a Team

▲

Death by Meeting

▲

Silos, Politics, and Turf Wars

Overcoming the Five Dysfunctions of a Team

Overcoming the Five Dysfunctions of a Team

A FIELD GUIDE

FOR LEADERS, MANAGERS, AND FACILITATORS

▲

PATRICK LENCIONI

JOSSEY-BASS
A Wiley Imprint
www.josseybass.com

Published by Jossey-Bass
A Wiley Imprint
989 Market Street, San Francisco, CA 94103-1741 www.josseybass.com

Jossey-Bass books and products are available through most bookstores. To contact Jossey-Bass directly call our Customer Care Department within the U.S. at 800-956-7739, outside the U.S. at 317-572-3986, or fax 317-572-4002.

Jossey-Bass also publishes its books in a variety of electronic formats. Some content that appears in print may not be available in electronic books.

Library of Congress Cataloging-in-Publication Data

Lencioni, Patrick, 1965-
Overcoming the five dysfunctions of a team : a field guide for leaders, managers, and facilitators / Patrick Lencioni.— 1st ed.
p. cm.
Includes bibliographical references.
ISBN 0-7879-7637-7 (alk. paper)
1. Teams in the workplace. I. Title.
HD66.L457 2005
658.4'022-dc22
2004025529

Printed in the United States of America
FIRST EDITION
PB Printing 10 9 8 7 6

CONTENTS

This book is dedicated to our

Table Group clients—who make all of this possible

and whom we appreciate more than we can say

WHY A FIELD GUIDE?

A year after *The Five Dysfunctions of a Team* was published, I received the welcome news that sales figures had exceeded initial expectations. That was good. But I had been warned that those numbers might begin to tail off in year two, and so, like most authors, I just hoped they wouldn't drop too drastically.

Well, you can imagine how pleasantly surprised I was to learn that instead of decreasing, sales of the book actually increased during the next twelve months. That was great.

But something else happened that I hadn't exactly expected; inquiries to my consulting firm, The Table Group, grew faster than we could have imagined, with readers calling to find out how they could better understand and implement the concepts in the book.

As wonderful as that may sound, it quickly became apparent to us that we could not help even a fraction of the readers who called us, and as a result, some of them might not feel comfortable diving into the process of improving their teams without a little more guidance. That was not so good, and therein lies the inspiration for this field guide.

The purpose of this little book is simple: to provide managers, team leaders, consultants, and other practitioners with a practical tool for helping implement the concepts in *The Five Dysfunctions of a Team*.

As with my other books, I decided to keep this one relatively short because time is the most precious commodity for most leaders, and learning to build a team, as important as it is, need not be exceedingly time-consuming or complicated. I've also tried to write and organize it in a way that will make it both readable on its own and easily accessible as a reference tool.

I sincerely hope that it is helpful to you and your team. Good luck!

PATRICK LENCIONI, *Lafayette, California, January 2005*

Overcoming the Five Dysfunctions of a Team

SECTION ONE

Getting Clear on the Concept

Because *teamwork* is a word that is used so loosely and frequently, it seems like a good idea to clarify exactly what I'm referring to when I talk about becoming a more cohesive team. That's what this section is about.

THE CASE FOR TEAMWORK

Building an effective, cohesive team is extremely hard. But it's also simple.

What I mean is that teamwork doesn't require great intellectual insights or masterful tactics. More than anything else, it comes down to courage and persistence.

And so, if you're committed to making your team a healthy one, and you can get the rest of the team to share your commitment, you're probably going to make it. And just in case you're not sure this will be worth the time and effort—and risk—let me make a case for going forward.

Teamwork remains the one sustainable competitive advantage that has been largely untapped.

I honestly believe that in this day and age of informational ubiquity and nanosecond change, teamwork remains the one sustainable competitive advantage that has been largely untapped. In the course of my career as a consultant to executives and their teams, I can say confidently that teamwork is almost always lacking within organizations that fail, and often present within those that succeed.

So why don't we hear more about the competitive importance of teamwork from business scholars and journalists? And why do so many leaders focus most of their time on other topics like finance, strategy, technology, and marketing?

First, because teamwork is hard to measure. Why? Because it impacts the outcome of an organization in such comprehensive and invasive ways that it's virtually impossible to isolate it as a single variable. Many executives prefer solutions that are more easily measurable and verifiable, and so they look elsewhere for their competitive advantages.

But even if the impact of teamwork were more easily measurable, executives probably would still look elsewhere. Why? Because teamwork is extremely hard to achieve. It can't be bought, and it can't be attained by hiring an intellectual giant from the world's best business school. It requires levels of courage and discipline—and emotional energy—that even the most driven executives don't always possess.

As difficult as teamwork is to measure and achieve, its power cannot be denied. When people come together and set aside their individual needs for the good of the whole, they can accomplish what might have looked impossible on paper. They do this by eliminating the politics and confusion that plague most organizations. As a result, they get more done in less time and with less cost. I think that's worth a lot of effort.

One more thing is worth mentioning. When it comes to helping people find fulfillment in their work, there is nothing more important than teamwork. It gives people a sense of connection and belonging, which ultimately makes them better parents, siblings, friends, and neighbors. And so building better teams at work can—

and usually does—have an impact that goes far beyond the walls of your office or cubicle.

So what are we waiting for? Let's get started.

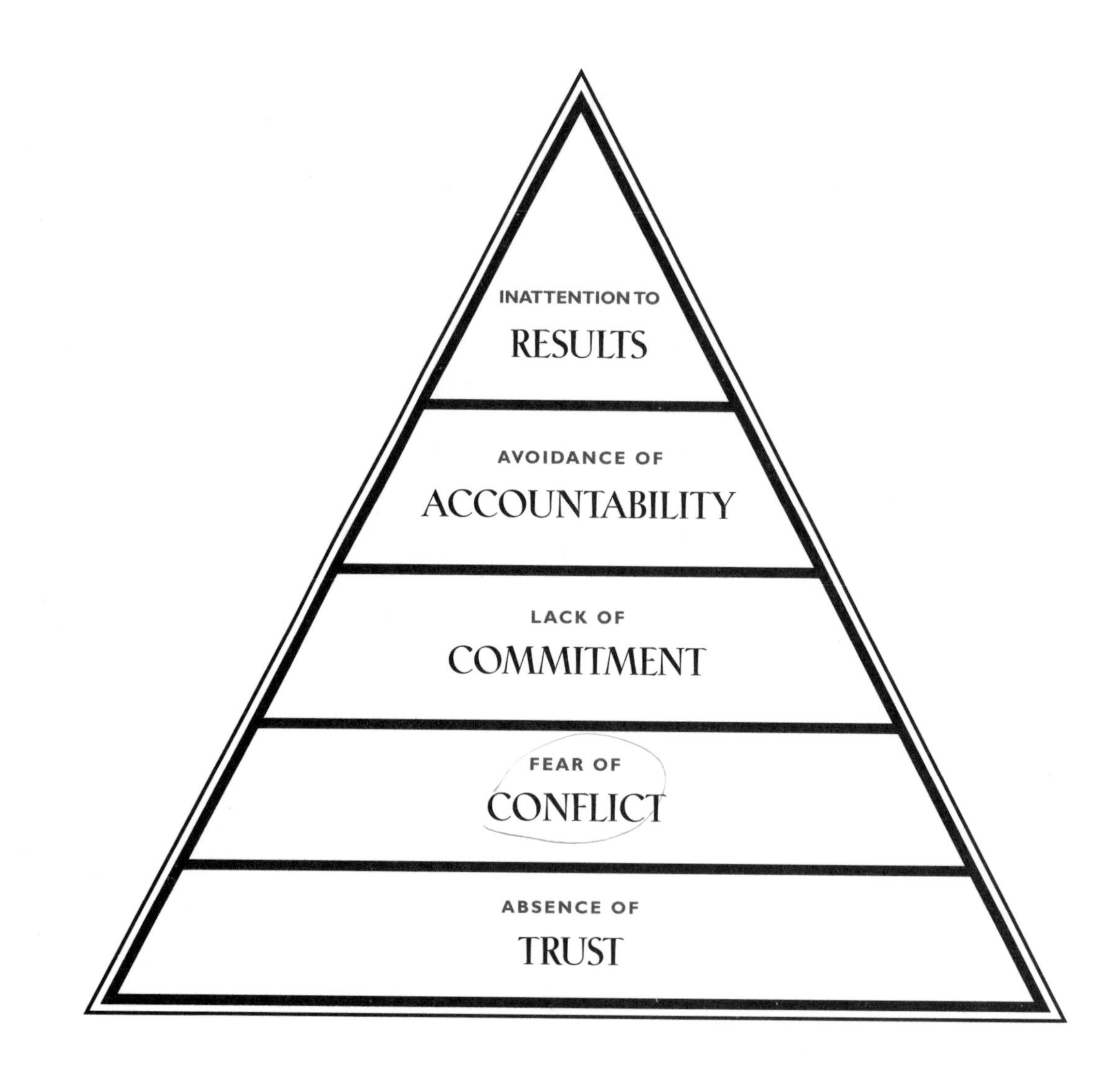

THE FIVE DYSFUNCTIONS OF A TEAM

A QUICK OVERVIEW OF THE MODEL

As difficult as teamwork can be to achieve, it is not complicated. And so, if I can't describe it in a page or two, then I've probably made it too complex. Here goes.

The true measure of a team is that it accomplishes the results that it sets out to achieve. To do that on a consistent, ongoing basis, a team must overcome the five dysfunctions listed here by embodying the behaviors described for each one.

- **Dysfunction #1: Absence of Trust:** Members of great teams trust one another on a fundamental, emotional level, and they are comfortable being vulnerable with each other about their weaknesses, mistakes, fears, and behaviors. They get to a point where they can be completely open with one another, without filters. This is essential because ...
- **Dysfunction #2: Fear of Conflict:** ... teams that trust one another are not afraid to engage in passionate dialogue around issues and decisions that are key to the organization's success. They do not hesitate to disagree with, challenge, and question one another, all in the spirit of finding the best answers, discovering the truth, and making great decisions. This is important because ...
- **Dysfunction #3: Lack of Commitment** ... teams that engage in unfiltered conflict are able to achieve genuine buy-in around important decisions, even when various members of the team initially disagree. That's because they ensure that all opinions and ideas are put on the table and considered, giving confidence to team members that no stone has been left unturned. This is critical because ...
- **Dysfunction #4: Avoidance of Accountability:** ... teams that commit to decisions and standards of performance do not hesitate to hold one another accountable for adhering to those decisions and standards. What is more, they don't rely on the team leader as the primary source of accountability, they go directly to their peers. This matters because ...
- **Dysfunction #5: Inattention to Results:** ... teams that trust one another, engage in conflict, commit to decisions, and hold one another accountable are very likely to set aside their individual needs and agendas and focus almost exclusively on what is best for the team. They do not give in to the temptation to place their departments, career aspirations, or ego-driven status ahead of the collective results that define team success.

That's it.

▲

TWO IMPORTANT QUESTIONS

Before embarking on a team-building effort, your team needs to answer two big questions:

Question #1: Are we really a team?

Sometimes a team improvement effort is doomed from the start because the group going through it isn't really a team at all, at least not in the true sense of the word. You see, a team is a relatively small number of people (anywhere from three to twelve) that shares common goals as well as the rewards and responsibilities for achieving them. Team members readily set aside their individual or personal needs for the greater good of the group.

If your "team" doesn't meet these criteria, you might want to consider whether you have a smaller subset of the group that is a real team. Or maybe the group is simply a collection of people who report to the same manager, but with relatively little interdependence and mutual accountability (that is, not a team).

And remember, it's okay to decide that your group isn't a team. In a world where teamwork is rarer than we might think, plenty of non-teams succeed. In fact, if your group is not meant to be a team, it's far better to be clear about that than to waste time and energy pretending you're something you're not. Because that only creates false expectations, which leads to frustration and resentment.

Question #2: Are we ready for heavy lifting?

Having said all that (in question #1), let me be very clear: the advantages of being a true team are enormous. But they can't be achieved without a willingness to invest considerable time and emotional energy in the process. Unfortunately, many teams aren't prepared for this, and try to take shortcuts and half measures. Not only does this prevent them from making progress, it can actually lead to a decrease in the team's performance.

It's important that you go into this process with eyes wide open, and with no illusions about what is required. That doesn't mean becoming a team takes years, or that it will be unpleasant. In fact, most teams can make significant progress in weeks or months, and find the process itself to be one of the most rewarding parts of their professional lives. If they do it right. Let's talk about how to do just that.

SECTION TWO

Overcoming the Five Dysfunctions of a Team

Okay, this is the meat of the book, the part where I go through the dysfunctions and explain what they mean, how you can help your team overcome them, and which tools and exercises my colleagues and I find to be most useful. A detailed explanation of the tools and exercises mentioned in these segments can be found in Section Four.

OVERCOMING DYSFUNCTION #1

BUILDING TRUST

Based on my experience working with teams during the past ten years or so, I've come to one inescapable conclusion: no quality or characteristic is more important than trust. In fact, my work with teams revolves around trust more than any other topic, and that's why this is the longest, most important section in this book.

No quality or characteristic is more important than trust.

Unfortunately, there is probably no quality or characteristic that is as rare as trust, either. But I suppose that's good news for your team, because if you can be the first on your block to build trust, the possibility of achieving a real competitive advantage is great.

So why is trust so rare? Two reasons. First, people use the word inconsistently, and so *trust* means different things to different people. Second, because it's just plain hard. Let's start by defining what we mean by trust, and the best way to do that is to clarify what trust is *not*.

Defining Trust

Trust is not the ability of team members to predict one another's behaviors because they've known each other for a long time. Even the most dysfunctional teams, or families for that matter, can learn to forecast one another's words and actions based on observable patterns over a long period of time. So when, for example, a person says, "I trust that Bob will start swearing at me if I mention his inability to arrive at a meeting on time," know that this is not the kind of trust I'm talking about.

When it comes to teams, trust is all about vulnerability. Team members who trust one another learn to be comfortable being open, even exposed, to one another around their failures, weaknesses, even fears. Now, if this is beginning to sound like some get-naked, touchy-feely theory, rest assured that it is nothing of the sort.

People who aren't afraid to admit the truth about themselves are not going to engage in the kind of political behavior that wastes everyone's time and energy.

Vulnerability-based trust is predicated on the simple—and practical—idea that people who aren't afraid to admit the truth about themselves are not going to engage in the kind of political behavior that wastes everyone's time and energy, and more important, makes the accomplishment of results an unlikely scenario.

Here's an example of how damaging a lack of trust can be in an organization.

The Invulnerable Leader Story

I once worked with a large company—one that, if you haven't used their products, you've certainly heard of—that demonstrated how a lack of trust can destroy years of hard work and accomplishment. Let's call the company Passivity.

Passivity had been a highly respected and accomplished company over the years, but had recently fallen on hard times at the hands of a larger, more aggressive competitor. Still, the company had legions of dedicated customers and employees, if not Wall Street analysts.

Enter the new CEO of Passivity, a man who neither valued nor elicited trust among his executive team. As the company, under the guidance of its new leader, watched its demise accelerate, journalists and industry-watchers attributed the spiral to unwise decisions about products and strategy. And while those decisions certainly contributed to the problem, they were merely symptoms of a bigger issue.

That issue could only be observed behind the scenes, at executive staff meetings. It was there that a tornado of distrust was raging, leaving in its wake a sea of bad decisions and real human suffering. Not to mention drowning stock options.

As is often the case, the trust vacuum emanated from the leader, a brilliant man whose intelligence was rivaled only by his inability to acknowledge his own limitations. This was made apparent to me, and the rest of his team, on many occasions, but none more painfully so than when he reluctantly "shared" the results of his 360-degree feedback during a staff meeting.

Standing before his team with his 360-degree report in his hands, the leader of Passivity started by addressing his weaknesses. "It says here that I'm not a good listener," he announced, with a puzzled look on his face. "Hmm. What do you guys think?" After a brief and awkward moment of silence, the executives around the table assured their boss that he was not a bad listener at all, and that he was indeed better than many of the other leaders they had known. He accepted their reassurance without a fight.

"Okay. What about this next one? It says I don't give enough praise." Again, one by one the team shrugged and nodded their assurance that this was not really a problem.

It was at that moment that I kindly reminded the team that they were, in fact, the only people who had completed the 360-degree survey, and that someone had to have given the CEO low scores in these areas. After an awkward pause, a lone brave soul raised his hand. "Okay, I'll admit it. I think you could give a little more positive feedback," he offered almost apologetically. "I mean, my people don't usually hear anything from you unless they've screwed up. It would be nice if we, or they, knew what they were doing well."

After yet another awkward moment, one of the other executives in the room declared, in the direction of the CEO, "I don't see it. I think you give more praise than most CEOs I know." This set off a wave of head nodding, leaving the lone brave soul out in the cold, wondering why he'd bothered telling the truth.

As humorously pathetic as this example may seem, I am afraid to admit that it actually happened, proving again that truth is stranger than fiction. What it illustrates is the difficulty that people have in admitting their weaknesses, their faults, their mistakes, even when there is *real data* indicating otherwise.

Of course the real point of this story is not what actually happened that day. It is what it created. The members of that team learned a lesson: don't be vulnerable. After all, if the CEO isn't capable of being honest about his own issues, why should his direct reports fess up about theirs?

And so, the executives at Passivity learned to engage in a remarkable game of masquerade, pretending to know things that they didn't and to search for solutions to their problems only in places that wouldn't reflect poorly on them or their departments. Remarkably, as the company's results tanked, the resilience of the leaders' invulnerability held firm. Today, the company is a shell of what it once was, having lost most of its leaders and many of the employees who built the firm. A few years ago it was sold to another company and exists now in name only.

When journalists write the epitaphs of companies like Passivity, they cite unwise strategic decisions and product defects. But if they really wanted to understand the root causes of their failure, they would look at the inability of executive team members to be vulnerable with one another—to build trust.

The Difficulty of Vulnerability-Based Trust

The second reason why vulnerability-based trust is so rare is that it is just plain hard to achieve, even when teams understand the definition. That's because human beings, especially the adult variety, have this crazy desire for self-preservation. The idea of putting themselves at risk for the good of others is not natural, and is rarely rewarded in life, at least not in the ways that most people expect.

So we learn things like "look out for number one" or "don't let 'em see you sweat" or whatever other cliché calls for us to think of ourselves before others. And while this may be wise counsel if you're in prison, on a team it's lethal.

The key to all of this, then, is to teach team members to get comfortable being exposed to one another, unafraid to honestly say things like "I was wrong" and "I made a mistake" and "I need help" and "I'm not sure" and "you're better than I am at that" and yes, even "I'm sorry." If team members cannot bring themselves to readily speak these words when the situation calls for it, they aren't going to learn to trust one another. Instead, they're going to waste time and energy thinking about what they *should* say, and wondering about the true intentions of their peers.

The key ingredient to building trust is not time. It is courage.

Now, as hard as it is to achieve vulnerability-based trust, it is entirely doable. And better yet, it doesn't have to take a lot of time. In fact, I've seen remarkable distrust on teams that have worked together for years and years, and I've seen teams that have been together for six months develop amazing amounts of trust. No, the key ingredient is not time. It is courage.

For a team to establish real trust, team members, beginning with the leader, must be willing to take risks without a guarantee of success. They will have to be vulnerable without knowing whether that vulnerability will be respected and reciprocated.

TOOLS AND EXERCISES

The Personal Histories Exercise

As in most self-improvement programs, it's best to start small. The point of the first exercise is simply to help people get comfortable with moderate vulnerability. My colleagues and I have done it with virtually every team we work with, and I have to admit, I'm always worried that it's not going to work. And every time, it does.

Here's how it goes.

At a staff meeting or off-site, go around the room and have every member of the team explain three things: where they grew up, how many kids were in their family, and what was the most difficult or important challenge of their childhood (but not their *inner* childhood; just the most important challenge of being a kid!).

Now, I mentioned that I'm always afraid the exercise is not going to work, and I suppose that's because I think that most people who work on teams already know one another and are not going to learn anything new from this exercise. And then, twenty minutes later, I always find that people are shocked about what they didn't know about their peers.

I've heard the most amazing stories during the Personal Histories Exercise. Like the one about the guy who grew up in Chicago and didn't have indoor plumbing (this was in the sixties!). And the guy who moved out of his home at age thirteen and started a business. And then there are the numerous people who moved around their entire lives, or grew up without parents, or had eight siblings, or none.

Personal Histories Story #1

I worked with a team that had been together for a number of years, and when it came time for one particular guy to explain his biggest challenge of childhood, he hesitated for a moment and then explained that when he was eight years old, his twelve-year-old brother was murdered, and that was tough on him. One of his teammates sitting across the table from this guy was stunned, and after a moment said, "I've worked with you for nine years and I never heard about that." To which his colleague said, "Yeah, I was just never sure about the right time to bring it up."

In case you're wondering whether this exercise is designed to provide me with some sort of fodder for cocktail parties, let me be clear about the purpose: when team members reveal aspects of their personal lives to their peers, they learn to get comfortable being open with them about other things. They begin to let down their guard about their strengths, weaknesses, opinions, and ideas.

And if this sounds manipulative, well, I guess it is. But in a good kind of way, like when I coax my son to sit in the shallow end of the pool so that he gets comfortable with the idea of going deeper and deeper until he swims. People need to feel the gradual progress of opening up to their peers before diving in too deep.

Asking them to be too vulnerable too quickly is not only unfair, it often provokes a resistance that is hard to overcome later. Which is why I don't throw my son in the deep end of the pool cold turkey, I suppose.

Now, there's another side-benefit to the Personal Histories Exercise. In addition to helping people open up, it helps everyone else overcome one of the great destroyers of teamwork.

The *fundamental attribution error* is simply this: human beings tend to falsely attribute the negative behaviors of others to their character (an internal attribution), while they attribute their own negative behaviors to their environment (an external attribution). Why? Because we like to believe that we do bad things because of the situations we are in, but somehow we easily come to the conclusion that others do bad things because they are predisposed to being bad. (Similarly, we often attribute other people's success to their environment and our own success to our character. That's because we like to believe that we are inherently good and talented, while others are merely lucky, beneficiaries of good fortune.)

Asking team members to be too vulnerable too quickly is not only unfair, it often provokes a resistance that is hard to overcome later.

By going through the Personal Histories Exercise, team members come to understand one another at a more fundamental level; they learn how they became the people they are today. As a result, there is a far greater likelihood that empathy and understanding will trump judgment and accusation when it comes to interpreting questionable behavior.

Personal Histories Story #2

I once worked with a woman who didn't seem to get along with her peers on an executive team. She rarely smiled or made eye contact. Her colleagues had come to the conclusion that she didn't like them and that she didn't want to collaborate with them, until we did the Personal Histories Exercise. "Okay," she began cautiously. "I grew up the only child of a three-star general who was a rigid disciplinarian. We lived overseas for most of my childhood. I became a world-class concert violinist, but whenever I received recognition or awards for my music, my dad would try to knock me down a peg or two so that I didn't get a big head."

It was as though she had just revealed she was a Martian; suddenly everyone now had something they could attribute her behavior to, other than her dislike for them.

For instance, when the CFO of a company questions an item on an employee's expense report, colleagues on an executive team might jump to the conclusion that the motivation is one of control or lack of trust. When those colleagues understand, for instance, that the CFO grew up in a poor family or with extremely conservative parents, they might be more likely to understand the real motivation. That's not to say they won't question the CFO and lobby for more resources. But it is to say that they'll do it with a fairer and more accurate understanding of where their colleague is coming from.

One of the keys to making the Personal Histories Exercise work is to anticipate the initial objections of team participants. When I introduce the exercise to senior executives, I assure them that I'm not interested in their inner child or their deepest, darkest secrets. I also assure them that this is the only exercise we'll do that could even be remotely associated with anything touchy-feely. Then, when then they complete the twenty-minute assignment, they're pleasantly surprised by its lack of pretension, and more important, by the fact that they understand their peers better than they had just a half hour earlier.

One of the keys to making the Personal Histories Exercise work is to anticipate the initial objections of team participants.

Another key to a successful exercise is proper facilitation. This can be a little delicate because the issues at hand are sometimes, well, delicate. For instance, a couple of people out of every ten we take through the exercise will report that they're unable to think of any difficulties from their childhood. While occasionally this seems to be the result of not wanting to open up to the group, most of the time they seem genuinely stumped. "I just had a wonderful childhood," they'll confess sheepishly. "My parents loved us, we weren't rich or poor, we all got along well . . ." Of course, that's fine.

On the other hand, it isn't uncommon that one or two members of a team will disclose something particularly sensitive. The alcoholism of a parent. The death of a sibling or friend. A difficult family relationship. It is important for a facilitator to demonstrate focused listening and respectful appreciation during these moments. Sometimes the best way to do that is to allow a quiet moment to pass after the story, smile at the person who shared their story, and just say thank you.

For those of you freaking out right about now as you consider having to hear someone disclose some painful, jarring memory and break out into uncontrollable tears, rest assured that we rarely—no, make that never—have had this occur. No one has said something that was downright inappropriate, and thankfully, we've never had someone respond inappropriately either. Human beings, by and large, are good, and other than an occasionally clueless individual, they almost always treat one another with respect.

If—and I mean *if*—someone falls far short of these expectations for being a reasonable human being, might I suggest that you consider whether this isn't a red flag about their overall membership on the team? Just a thought.

A few final thoughts on the Personal Histories Exercise. I suppose you can choose different questions to ask. Like a person's first job, or worst job, or biggest mistake or most influential leader in their life. The key is that the questions elicit a response that calls for a person to reveal something personal and relevant. And not silly. Also, it's best if people's responses are relatively similar in length. Probably a minute or two, at most. However, this is an exercise you don't want to manage too closely, because cutting people off or interrupting is particularly bad during this kind of conversation.

Okay, the Personal Histories Exercise is good for helping people get comfortable being vulnerable and better understanding one another. But the real breakthroughs in terms of vulnerability and trust come when you introduce a behavioral profiling tool that allows team members to accurately and openly assess their strengths and weaknesses.

Behavioral Profiling

The idea here is simple: give team members an objective, reliable means for understanding and describing one another. This provides two powerful benefits.

First, it drastically increases the likelihood that team members will admit their weaknesses and strengths to one another. After all, once they voluntarily self-identify their "type," they have little reason to resist opening up. In fact, I've found that they're usually eager and relieved to tell their peers who they are and why they act the way they do.

Second, by providing team members with a common vocabulary for describing their differences and similarities, you make it safe for them to give each other feedback without feeling like they're making accusatory or unfounded generalizations. It is amazing to observe previously guarded team members calling out one another's strengths and weaknesses after having those strengths and weaknesses validated by an objective tool.

It is amazing to observe previously guarded team members calling out one another's strengths and weaknesses after having those strengths and weaknesses validated by an objective tool.

Now there are many profiling tools out there, such as the DiSC, the Social Style Model, RightPath Profiles, and Insights, and I suppose that all of them have their own advantages. However, my recommended favorite, and the one we use most often at

The Table Group, is the Myers-Briggs Type Indicator (MBTI). Here's why.

First, and most important, the MBTI is valid and reliable. It has been tested for decades since its development in the 1940s by Isabel Briggs Myers, based on the insights of her mother, Katherine Cook Briggs. The amount of research and testing that has been done is staggering.

Second, the MBTI is the most widely known tool out there. Normally that would make me somewhat skeptical, as I wouldn't want people to do something just because everyone else is. But in this case, the popularity of the tool is important. That's because most of the executives we work with (more than 70 percent) are somewhat familiar with the MBTI and have taken part in a Myers-Briggs exercise at some point in their careers. And so they tend to accept its validity relatively quickly and can get up to speed with less time and effort than they'd spend on something new. Having to convince them to adopt the latest, greatest theory being developed by astrological surfers at U.C. Berkeley is going to severely reduce your chances of success.

Another benefit of the popularity of the MBTI is the established vocabulary that exists among many—if not most—of the leaders we meet. Sometimes within minutes of beginning a discussion of Myers-Briggs, someone will say "I'm an ENTJ" and everyone around the room will nod their heads in unison and say "no wonder!"

Advice on Administering the MBTI

As good a tool as the MBTI is—and I suppose what I'm about to say applies to any tool, for that matter—the way it is administered is critical to its success. (That's probably why a certified or qualified instructor is required.) A great tool done poorly will fail. A poor tool done well will probably fail too. I guess the only thing to do is pick a good tool and do it well. Here are some tips:

1. *Go fast.* People are generally smart, and there is nothing like a slow lecture or a simplistic exercise to entice them to tune out and check their Blackberries for messages. When in doubt, go faster and leave things out rather than being overly concerned with covering everything up front. Better that they ask questions later for clarification than get bored.
2. *Apply it to work.* Every profiling tool is going to be based on a psychological, behavioral theory, but the reason why you're talking to your clients or employees about it is so they can build trust and become a more highly functioning team at work. So don't bore them, or even indulge them, in too much theory. If someone in the room wants a lot of theory (and often there is someone who does—which tells you something about their Myers-Briggs type), then refer them to a book or Web site and move on. Get back to what all of this has to do with the way the team works.
3. *Anticipate objections.* Don't wait for someone to say, "This is a bunch of touchy-feely mumbo jumbo!" Instead, start by saying,

"Now for those of you who might be wondering if this is a bunch of touchy-feely mumbo jumbo, let me say right now that I wondered the same thing when I first learned about this. And I can tell you, it is based in real data and it is extremely practical for what we're trying to do here . . ." Something like that. You get the picture. Demonstrate to your audience that you know, and even understand, what they might be thinking, and take the issue off the table. It's simple—but surprisingly effective.

4. *Know your stuff cold.* That doesn't mean you have to impress people by showing them that you know your stuff cold. But it will help when there is push-back, or when someone (usually an ENTP) tries to debate the merits of whatever tool you're using.

My colleagues and I have had so many powerful experiences using the Myers-Briggs that it's hard to choose one or two to describe here. But here is a typical one.

Behavioral Profiling Story

We facilitated an off-site with a team of executives from one of America's largest and most respected transportation companies. The average age in the room was higher than at most companies we work with, and as it turned out, we had the rare occasion to work with a team whose members were not terribly familiar with the Myers-Briggs.

Now, this particular team hadn't yet become a real team; they were a collection of executives who had been amassed through acquisi-

tions and reorganizations. Most of them felt their main sense of allegiance to the teams they led in their former companies, and didn't feel particularly loyal to the men and women sitting in the room with us on that day.

In fact, it was worse than that. A few of them were actively trying to avoid giving up autonomy to the group, and were committed to retaining their own control. In short, there was little trust among them.

Each member of the group had taken twenty minutes or so prior to our off-site meeting to complete an online Myers-Briggs assessment, but we didn't give them their results until later in the session. Instead, we spent the first half hour explaining the theory behind the Myers-Briggs and having everyone qualitatively assess themselves by answering a series of questions. This allowed them to make their first guesses at their types.

Then we had them assess themselves again, this time by reading about something called "Temperament," which is based on the same theory as the Myers-Briggs. You might think that they'd already be growing impatient with yet another assessment, but it always amazes me how much people like to learn about themselves. They were now locked in the struggle of trying to figure out exactly who they were.

Now, still less than an hour into the session, we handed out the results of their online assessments, and asked them to compare those results with the two they had just completed, to see if a pattern was beginning to emerge. Finally, we handed out a MBTI reference book that contains, among other things, one-page descriptions of each of the sixteen types.

It was at this point that some of the executives started saying things like "Wow, where did you get this? This is amazing." And, "This really nailed me. I hope my wife doesn't see this." Some of them just laughed in an emotional sort of way at how accurately Mrs. Myers and Mrs. Briggs had figured them out.

But of course, some of the executives still hadn't identified their type, or at least not with conviction. And so we asked them questions and suggested they read descriptions of some of the other types in the reference book.

It is worth noting that no one in the room was questioning the validity of the tool at this point; they were all trying to apply it to themselves. And they were, every last one of them, having fun.

Okay, now we'd been at this for almost two hours, and so we called the question. "What are your types?" We went around the room, starting with the team leader, and then with those people who were most confident of having identified their types, and had them read aloud their one-page MBTI descriptions. Here's where, as always, it got really fun.

I will never get tired of watching the reticence and guardedness of untrusting teammates melt away as they acknowledge to one another what makes them tick. Without fail, there is laughter, teasing, relief, and insight. And that is exactly when the seeds of trust begin to grow.

In this particular case, one of the quieter members of the group, someone who had perhaps the most reasons to resist giving up autonomy to the team, blew his prospective teammates away with his description of his own type. Half the room was smiling as they listened, nodding as if to say "Aha!" The others were frowning, and when the two-minute reading was over, they said, "I don't see you that way."

This is common because in many cases, team members don't see the qualities that their colleague has just described precisely because that colleague hasn't been open or comfortable demonstrating them. In this case, the executive said, "No, this is definitely who I am. I'm actually more sensitive than you guys know." We then pointed out that because this guy has an introverting preference and a feeling preference, he tended to keep his emotions to himself. In fact, the team often thought he was holding back on purpose, and hiding his political motives. When they realized that it was just his natural behavioral tendency that caused this, they were amazed. And relieved.

Similarly, another guy on the team was something called an ENFJ, which often indicates an emotionally excitable and passionate style. As soon as the group heard him read his type, they started laughing. "No wonder you're always being so dramatic!" they good-naturedly teased. It was as though they were seeing him for the first time for who he really was.

Then, the CEO read his type to the team. "It says here I'm impatient. That's definitely true." The room howled in laughter. "Okay, okay," the CEO admitted. "I'm extremely impatient." That provoked a lighthearted but important discussion of how he was able to shut down conversation by giving people "the look." He went on to explain that he didn't want to bring discussions to a premature end, but that he just didn't know how to contain his desire for closure. The team agreed to push back more when this happened.

Now, after everyone had read their types, we plotted the entire team's collective profile on the white board so they could see what elements of their MBTI types were generally shared, and which were missing. The insights into the collective behavior of the team, and their resulting exposures, were substantial.

After approximately two and a half hours of discussion and exercise around the Myers-Briggs, we moved on, not wanting to allow people to get impatient with the theory. But we kept the list of the team's types on the wall for reference, knowing that it would be referred to again and again throughout the remainder of the off-site.

After the first day of an off-site, we usually ask team members to do a little homework. During the evening, we have them take a half hour or so to read a thorough description of their behavioral type, and then come prepared the next day to report on the three or four areas that they felt were particularly insightful about their style.

We also ask team members to identify one particular insight from their profile that they feel highlights a weakness that they would like to address for the good of the team. It is amazing to hear them call out behavioral issues about themselves that their peers would have struggled to raise.

By the time an off-site has ended, a team will have come to know one another in a deeper, more meaningful way than ever. And they'll be feeling somewhat bonded to one another. Unfortunately, when they get back to work, some of this is bound to disappear in the business of day-to-day work.

And that is precisely why it is critical to keep the Myers-Briggs and other profile-related learnings alive. There are a number of ways you can do this.

Maintaining Momentum

You can e-mail everyone a list of the team members' types. This is helpful because if they don't remember one another's profiles, they aren't going to be able to use them.

You should also encourage, or even require, that team members keep any reference material or collateral from the session on their desks back at work, rather than in a drawer or on a bookshelf. This increases the likelihood that they'll refer to it later, and that others will ask them about it.

And we always have team members go back to their direct reports and share their profile information. This serves three purposes. First, it provides a great opportunity for demonstrating vulnerability with their subordinates. Second, it gives those subordinates real insights into their leaders, so that they'll feel more comfortable providing feedback and interpreting behavior correctly. Third, it helps the executives develop a better understanding of their own profiles, because teaching is one of the best ways of learning.

Beyond these initial steps, it's important that the team get together relatively soon after the initial off-site to discuss their types again, and how they've used the information back at work. As with any new information, if it is not put to use and discussed, it quickly grows stale. Even a thirty-minute session sometime within the first month after the off-site can be enough to keep the progress alive.

As with any new information, if it is not put to use and discussed, it quickly grows stale.

Now, occasionally we work with a team with a member who isn't interested, willing, or capable of vulnerability-based trust. This poses a challenge for a team. Another story is probably worth telling here.

The Unyielding Team Member Story

The head of sales for one particular executive team we worked with decided that vulnerability wasn't his thing. He announced to the team, "Listen, it took me years to trust my wife, so I wouldn't hold my breath waiting for me to trust you guys." Everyone laughed it off, but the CEO realized that this wasn't going to change without some work.

So, over the course of a few months (which he would later admit was a little too long), the CEO unsuccessfully pushed the sales VP

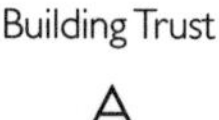

to open up to the team and earn their trust. Finally, he managed the reluctant executive out of the company, and was surprised to watch his team change almost overnight. The trust among the executives, and the speed and quality of their decisions, improved dramatically. All because of one person.

And that is a testament to the power of vulnerability, and the need for unanimity. Everyone on a team has to participate. That doesn't mean that everyone will do it the same way. But if even one member of a team is unwilling to be open about weaknesses, mistakes, and issues, it will have a profound impact on everyone else.

KEY POINTS—BUILDING TRUST

- Trust is the foundation of teamwork.
- On a team, trust is all about vulnerability, which is difficult for most people.
- Building trust takes time, but the process can be greatly accelerated.
- Like a good marriage, trust on a team is never complete; it must be maintained over time.

OVERCOMING DYSFUNCTION #2

MASTERING CONFLICT

Once a team has begun the process of building trust, it's time to think about leveraging that trust. That's right. Trust is important because it is a requirement for overcoming the next dysfunction, which is the all-too-common fear of conflict.

When I talk about conflict on a team, I'm talking about productive, ideological conflict: passionate, unfiltered debate around issues of importance to the team. Any team that wants to maximize its effectiveness needs to learn to do this, and doing so can only happen if vulnerability-based trust exists.

That's not to say that some teams that lack trust don't argue. It's just that their arguments are often destructive because they are laced with politics, pride, and competition, rather than humble pursuit of truth.

When people who don't trust one another engage in passionate debate, they are trying to win the argument. They aren't usually listening to the other person's ideas and then reconsidering their point of view; they're figuring out how to manipulate the conversation to get what they want. Or worse yet, they're not even arguing with the other person face-to-face but venting about them in the hallways after a meeting is over.

In contrast, when vulnerability-based trust exists, team members say everything that needs to be said, and there is nothing left to talk about behind closed doors.

The Inevitability of Discomfort

But this probably makes conflict sound too easy, too comfortable. The fact is, even among the best teams, conflict is always at least a little uncomfortable. No matter how clear everyone is that the conflict they're engaging in is focused on issues, not personalities, it is inevitable that they will feel under some degree of personal attack. It's just unrealistic for a person to say, "I'm sorry, Jan, but I don't agree with your approach to the project," and not expect Jan to feel some degree of personal rejection.

If team members are never pushing one another outside of their emotional comfort zones during discussions, then it is extremely likely that they're not making the best decisions for the organization.

But that is no reason to avoid conflict. In fact, if team members are not making one another uncomfortable at times, if they're never pushing one another outside of their emotional comfort zones during discussions, then it is extremely likely that they're not making the best decisions for the organization.

One way for a team to know if they are having enough conflict is for them to think about how an outsider to the team would feel sitting in on a team meeting. A great team will look at least a little strange to an outsider who isn't accustomed to the direct and unfiltered dialogue taking place. Like a friend invited to dinner at a close family's house, they would probably be a little taken aback, at least at first.

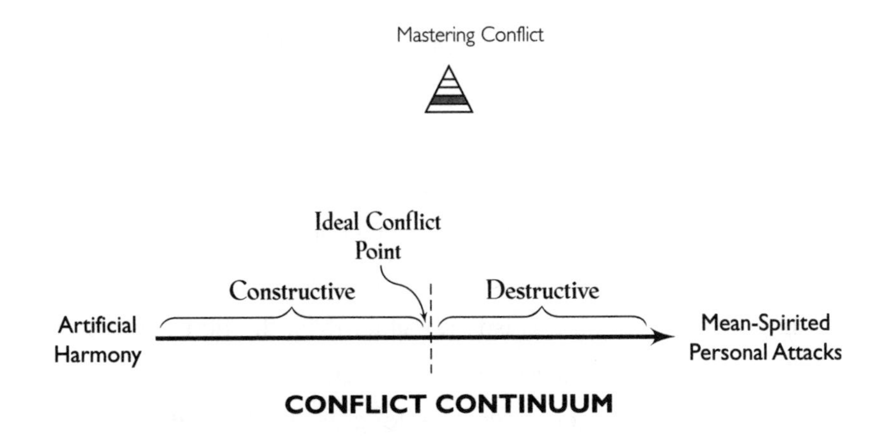

The Fear of Personal Conflict

Now, many people often ask me: "how do you avoid the conflict getting personal?" The answer has a few different angles. First, based on my experience working with hundreds of executive teams, it is extremely rare that people attack each other openly on a personal level. In fact, I can recall only a handful of incidents in which a teammate stepped over the line, and even in those cases, it was relatively mild. The bigger problem I see among most teams is that they never get close to anything remotely resembling personal conflict.

Think about conflict this way. Imagine a continuum. On one end, there is artificial harmony with no conflict at all, and on the other there are mean-spirited, personal attacks. In the exact middle of that continuum there is a line where conflict goes from constructive to destructive or vice versa, depending on which direction you're going. Now, the vast majority of teams I've encountered live close to the harmony end of the scale, fearing that any movement toward the middle is one step closer to murder.

Theoretically, the best place on the continuum is close to the middle, just to the left of the dividing line. This is the point where a team is having every bit of constructive conflict possible, without stepping over the line into destructive territory.

In reality, however, this isn't possible. Even the best teams will rarely but occasionally step over the line. And that's not only okay, it actually can be a good thing, as long as they're committed to working through it. Because when a team recovers from an incident of destructive conflict, it builds confidence that it can survive such an event, which in turn builds trust. This is not unlike a husband and wife recovering from a big argument and developing closer ties and greater confidence in their relationship as a result.

When a team recovers from an incident of destructive conflict, it builds confidence that it can survive such an event, which in turn builds trust.

TOOLS AND EXERCISES

Okay, enough theoretical stuff. Let's talk about practical ways to go about helping your team get more comfortable with productive conflict. And the first thing your team will want to do is determine its conflict profile.

Conflict Profiling

Yes, we're back to profiling again, but in a different way. In order to teach a team how to engage in productive conflict, it's important to understand everyone's viewpoints on and comfort levels with conflict, because they can differ radically.

On one extreme are the people who are comfortable screaming and shouting and arguing passionately; on the other are those who aren't comfortable airing the mildest of dissenting opinions out of fear of offending. It's important for the team to understand where people fall in this range, and why they fall there, so they can establish a conflict culture that everyone understands and adjusts to.

Someone's conflict profile is determined by a number of factors, not the least of which is their temperament or personality, which we talked about in the previous section, and we'll get into again in a moment. However, other factors like cultural background and family norms usually have a significant impact too.

In Japan, there is very little direct disagreement and debate during meetings. In Italy, emotional reactions will not be so rare. Even within a country there are differences. Cultural New Yorkers will tend to "get in one another's face" more than cultural Californians.

Of course, all of this can be trumped by family experience. Some people come from a background where parents and siblings rarely engaged in raw, emotional dialogue. Others watched their parents argue passionately, and then make up with equal passion. Which is better on a team? It doesn't matter. Regardless of whether a team tends to be more Japanese or Italian, New York or L.A., the only thing that really matters is this: are they holding back their opinions? Members of great teams do not.

But again, to get to that point, team members need to understand one another's conflict profiles. And it should come as no surprise that one of the best ways to accomplish this is to use a tool like the Myers-Briggs and others that address conflict styles.

The MBTI profile includes a very specific analysis about how each type deals with conflict. Having everyone on a team read their profile to their colleagues goes a long way toward clarifying the degree of difficulty of getting everyone on the same conflict page.

How does a team go about figuring out its collective conflict profile? Like so many other aspects of team-building—and life—the best way to do it is simply to talk about it. Ask everyone on the team to read their own conflict profiles in the Myers-Briggs book (or whatever other tool you're using), and then to discuss how that meshes with their personal views on conflict. Ask them to explain how their view of conflict was shaped by their childhood or maturation process.

When people self-identify and publicly declare their outlook on conflict, they become much more open to adjusting it to whatever team norms need to be established.

Most teams I've worked with are capable of accurate self-diagnosis: "Listen, in my family we never argued. I never saw my parents fight. I prefer to keep things at a nonemotional level, even if that means giving in." Or maybe it's: "I grew up with eight kids in my family, and so I learned how to dish it out and take it from my older brothers and sisters. I'm not afraid of a fight, and five minutes after it's over, there are no hard feelings." Or something in between.

The point here is that when people self-identify and publicly declare their outlook on conflict, they become much more open to adjusting it to whatever team norms need to be established.

Two other tools help teams identify their individual and collective conflict profile. One is the Thomas-Kilmann Conflict Mode Instrument—developed by two guys named Thomas and Kilmann, which makes it a pretty good name, don't you think? It depicts different approaches to interpersonal conflict based on the importance of the task at hand and the relationships of the people involved. We've provided a description of the model on page 131 in the "Tools and Exercises" segment.

The other is something we created at The Table Group, and it's also called the Thomas-Kilmann Instrument. No, that would be silly. We call it the Depth-Frequency Conflict Model, and it depicts how a team engages in conflict in terms of intensity and timing. It's also described on page 129 in the "Tools and Exercises" segment.

Conflict Norming

What does a conflict norm look like? It should probably entail rules of engagement, and these can vary drastically. On one hand, I've worked with teams where people like to get emotionally charged, use colorful language, and interrupt each other during debates. They've come to the conclusion that this is productive and acceptable, and so people don't get offended by it.

I've also known teams that try to keep discussions relatively objective and emotion-free. Which is better? That depends on the people involved. But one thing is certain: having clear norms gives teams a huge advantage when it comes to ensuring the exchange of good ideas.

Conflict Norming Story

I got to know an executive team that did a particularly good job setting conflict norms. They wanted a cohesive team so much—and understood how hard it is to achieve—that they drafted some-

thing they call the Team Effectiveness Charter. In it, they specified how they would engage one another. Among their various rules of engagement: "We will address conflict-laden issues, put on the table and get to the heart of issues about which we disagree or feel passionately. When discussing these issues, we will not withhold commentary . . ."

Every member of that team signed the Team Effectiveness Charter, and they bring it with them to meetings.

When it comes to establishing a norm for a team, a measure of judgment is required of a leader. While there is no doubt that the person in charge must set the tone based on a personal belief about what will lead to the best results for the organization, the leader also needs to take into account the capabilities and attitudes of the staff members. This is something of a balancing act.

Conflict Culture Story

I once worked with a team of automobile executives at a Japanese-American joint venture. Because the team was based in the United States, the predominant culture of the team was American. However, when it came time to engage in conflict and debate around sensitive issues, the team naturally allowed the Japanese members of the team to opt out of some of the exchanges. At times, they would ask them for their input in more general terms, and even then, there was much hemming and hawing and sucking of air through

teeth, which is common among Japanese executives who aren't accustomed to direct and lively back-and-forth during formal meetings.

Granted, this is an extreme case. For most teams, the differences in attitudes about conflict won't require such a drastic approach. In fact, in most situations a leader will simply have to ask some team members to stretch, stepping up to a little more conflict than they're used to, and others to ratchet down their tendency to be more emotional and demonstrative. The key to all of this is involving team members in establishing the norms, and then holding everyone accountable to what they've agreed upon.

(For more detail about establishing conflict norms, see page 123 in the "Tools and Exercises" segment.)

The leader is going to have to be ready to not only light the fuse of good conflict but to gently fan the flames for a while too.

Mining for Conflict

Okay, once a leader has been clear about wanting more productive conflict among team members, and the team has set norms for how to go about it, progress isn't going to come easily. That's because people who don't like conflict have an amazing ability to avoid it, even when they know it's theoretically necessary. (A cottage industry of psychotherapy is built around this phenomenon.)

So the leader is going to have to be ready to not only light the fuse of good conflict but to gently fan the flames for a while too. Here's what I mean.

Even when norms have been set, most people will shy away from conflict when they aren't accustomed to it. And that's why a team leader must become a miner of conflict. What does that mean? It means the leader must seek out opportunities for unearthing buried conflict and forcing team members to address those issues. In some cases, this means almost stirring the pot, but only when there is a good chance that a real issue needs to be uncovered.

Now, leaders who don't like conflict themselves might want to enlist the aid of the team members who are naturally more inclined toward mining. In any case, the key to mining is to ensure that important issues are not left beneath the surface but dug for like the buried treasure that they are.

Real-Time Permission

Even if a leader is adept at mining for conflict, there are still obstacles to overcome. That's because when a group of people who are not accustomed to having open, honest disagreement begin to do so, they are going to feel uncomfortable. Guilty, probably, too. And that is when a leader needs to do something that seems largely counterintuitive: interrupt.

As odd as it may sound, a leader should interrupt team members who are in the midst of an uncustomary debate, simply to remind them that what they are doing is okay. I've done this many times, sometimes with senior executives of large companies, and frankly, I always feel somewhat paternal doing it.

"Excuse me, CEO Johnson and CFO Smith. I just want to remind you both that this argument you're having, though uncomfortable, is exactly what we've been talking about. This is good. Keep going." Something like that, anyway.

That's when I think they're going to look at me and say, "We're adults, you idiot. Of course we know this is good."

But they don't. In fact—and this is the whole point—they actually seem relieved. They shed whatever momentary anxiety they were feeling and resume the debate in a more comfortable, confident manner.

I call it real-time permission because I don't think it's enough to give people theoretical permission to engage in conflict. In the heat of the moment, even the most self-disciplined people will often balk. But when you give them explicit permission precisely at the moment they need it, they take it more to heart, and you've provided a valuable teaching moment.

The lack of conflict is precisely the cause of one of the biggest problems that meetings have: they are boring.

Meetings and Conflict

For most teams, conflict is not something that happens every moment of the day. And indeed it shouldn't. However, there is one setting, or arena, where conflict must be apparent. Based on the subtitle of this section, you've probably already guessed that I'm talking about meetings.

But why is conflict so important at meetings? Because the lack of conflict is precisely the cause of one of the biggest problems that meetings have: they are boring. Ask a hundred employees to give you three words that describe meetings, and ninety-nine of them are going to say "boring"—and it will probably be their first response. And so, the questions we need to ask ourselves are these: Does it matter if meetings are boring? And do they have to be that way? The respective answers to these questions are yes and no.

Boring meetings are indeed a big problem. The ultimate penalty of boring meetings is bad decisions, not to mention wasted time. When team members lose interest during a meeting, they fail to surface critical opinions, and they do not fully evaluate whatever opinions are aired. Moreover, they probably aren't even putting the right issues on the table for discussion, because they're more interested in getting out of the meeting on time, having already accepted that meetings are a waste of time anyway.

But meetings are not hopeless. Team members can indeed become engaged in a meeting, but only when there is something at stake, a conflict worth caring about. It might be a conflict between the company and a competitor. Or a conflict over how to use scarce resources. Or a conflict about the best course of action to take to meet the needs of customers. And when team members passionately weigh in, suddenly the meeting gets interesting.

How does a leader go about nurturing good conflict during meetings? They take a lesson from movies. Like meetings, all great movies must have conflict. Either man versus man, like in *Rocky*. (I use "man" to include both men and women here.) Or man versus nature, like in *Jaws* or *The Perfect Storm*. Or man versus himself, like John Nash struggling with his sanity in *A Beautiful Mind*.

But it's not enough for a movie to have conflict. It has to give its audience a glimpse of that conflict right away. Screenwriters and directors refer to this as "the hook." And that takes place in the first ten minutes of every movie. When screenwriters or directors fail to hook an audience, they run the risk of losing people. And the same is true of meetings.

Team leaders must give members a reason to care at the beginning of a meeting or discussion. They must raise the anxiety of the team about why the issues about to be discussed matter, and what could go wrong if bad decisions are made. By doing so, they immediately get everyone engaged.

Of course, then they must mine for conflict, keeping the issue alive until it has been resolved. Just like a movie audience, people who invest their energy and passion in a difficult issue have a need to achieve clarity and resolution. And when they do, an amazing sense of accomplishment and commitment results. But I'm jumping ahead now. And besides, all of this is described in more detail in a book called *Death by Meeting,* which I also happened to write.

Conflict Resolution Obstacles

Okay, once you get your team more comfortable with conflict, you're going to find that they often struggle to achieve resolution around the issue they're discussing or debating. And while that is often a cue for you to step in and break a tie, in some cases it is the result of an obstacle having nothing to do with the issue itself.

What kind of obstacles am I talking about? Things like environmental obstacles (the physical environment where the conflict is taking place), relationship obstacles (an unresolved legacy event between the team members involved), and individual obstacles (an emotional or social deficiency on the part of one particular team member).

When these obstacles present themselves, it is critical for a team, and especially its leader, to identify the distraction—even if it cannot be worked out at that moment—before attempting to resolve the original issue at hand. What is important is that the obstacle is acknowledged so that it does not continue to cloud the conversation about the real issue. (For more information about conflict resolution obstacles, see the Conflict Resolution Model on page 124).

KEY POINTS—MASTERING CONFLICT

- Good conflict among team members requires trust, which is all about engaging in unfiltered, passionate debate around issues.
- Even among the best teams, conflict will at times be uncomfortable.
- Conflict norms, though they will vary from team to team, must be discussed and made clear among the team.
- The fear of occasional personal conflict should not deter a team from having regular, productive debate.

OVERCOMING DYSFUNCTION #3

ACHIEVING COMMITMENT

Like trust, conflict is important not in and of itself but because it enables a team to overcome the next dysfunction: the lack of commitment. And like its predecessors, commitment needs to be correctly defined before it can be achieved.

Teams that commit to decisions and standards do so because they know how to embrace two separate but related concepts: buy-in and clarity. Buy-in is the achievement of honest emotional support. Clarity is the removal of assumptions and ambiguity from a situation.

Commitment is about a group of intelligent, driven individuals buying in to a decision precisely when they *don't* naturally agree. In other words, it's the ability to defy a lack of consensus.

Buy-In

Let me be crystal clear about something: commitment is not consensus. Waiting for everyone on a team to agree intellectually on a decision is a good recipe for mediocrity, delay, and frustration, which is why it amazes me that so many of the teams I work with still seem determined to achieve consensus.

Ironically, commitment is something of the opposite. It's about a group of intelligent, driven individuals buying in to a decision precisely when they *don't* naturally agree. In other words, it's the ability to defy a lack of consensus.

The great teams I've worked with embrace disagreement and actually enjoy moments of temporary indecision. They take pleasure in making and rallying around and buying in to decisions when the "right" answer seems nowhere to be found.

The key to making this happen has everything to do with conflict—and leadership.

When a group of people know that their colleagues have no reservations about disagreeing with one another, and that every available opinion and perspective has been unapologetically aired, they will have the confidence to embrace a decision and abandon whatever their initial opinion might have been. But of course, this assumes that someone has to break the tie.

And that's one of the most critical roles of the leader. Good leaders drive commitment among the team by first extracting every possible idea, opinion, and perspective from the team. Then, comfortable that nothing has been left off the table, they must have the courage and wisdom to step up and make a decision, one that is sure to run counter to at least one of the team members, and usually more.

The amazing thing about this is that nineteen and a half times out of twenty, everyone sitting around that table will leave the room actively committed to implementing the solution that the leader has stipulated, even when that decision does not mesh with their own recommendation. Even when it is diametrically opposed!

How can this be possible? Because most human beings are drastically more reasonable than we think they are. In my work with teams, I've come to understand that most people don't really need to have their ideas adopted (a.k.a. "get their way") in order to buy in to a decision. They just want to have their ideas heard, understood, considered, and explained within the context of the ultimate decision.

Clarity

Unfortunately, even when teams master this ability to "disagree and commit" (this is something that the folks at Intel came up with years ago), they can still fail to benefit from their commitment. That's because many teams fail to achieve clarity and alignment around a decision. Instead, they make well-intentioned assumptions about what they've agreed to, and they end up creating confusion and frustration among employees who wonder whether their leaders are even talking to one another. I've seen this happen often and it's worth describing.

Most people don't really need to have their ideas adopted (a.k.a. "get their way") in order to buy in to a decision. They just want to have their ideas heard, understood, considered, and explained within the context of the ultimate decision.

Lack of Clarity Story

At a large technology company I worked with, the CEO and his team had a meeting to discuss how to respond to a downturn in the company's revenue. After two hours of discussion and debate, the team left the conference room with a decision: to freeze hiring until the company's bottom line had improved. The head of HR was charged with communicating the decision, and so she immediately sent out a note to all managers announcing the decision.

Within five minutes of the note being sent, three of the six executives who had attended that meeting went to her office claiming, "I didn't think that applied to my organization!" "We can't freeze hiring in Sales!" "That doesn't include Product Development, does it?!"

As this example demonstrates, commitment cannot occur if people are unclear about exactly what is being committed to. Unfortunately, this is not a rarity among many of the teams I've worked with.

It is amazing to me how a group of intelligent, highly educated adults, all of whom speak the same language, can sit in a room for two hours of discussion, and then leave the room under the false impression that everyone is on the same page.

TOOLS AND EXERCISES

This problem with failing to align around commitments can easily be avoided by using two simple techniques I call "Commitment Clarification" and "Cascading Communication." Here's how they work.

Commitment Clarification

With five minutes to go at the end of a meeting—any type of meeting—the leader of the team needs to call a question: *What exactly have we decided here today?* At the white board, the leader writes down the decisions that the group thinks it has made.

In many cases, team members see what the leader is writing on the board and react: "Wait a second. That's not what I thought we agreed on." And so the group dives back into the conversation until everyone is clear.

It is amazing to me how a group of intelligent, highly educated adults, all of whom speak the same language, can sit in a room for two hours of discussion, and then leave the room under the false impression that everyone is on the same page. Such is the nature of nuanced communication, I suppose.

In any case, by being extremely explicit about what has been agreed upon, a team will be able to identify discrepancies before a decision has been announced. Now, you might be wondering, "But maybe team members are purposefully sitting back and allowing for ambiguity, preferring to later ask for forgiveness rather than permission." Read on . . .

Cascading Communication

To avoid that situation, the leader must also engage in cascading communication. That means demanding that the team go back and communicate the decisions to their staff members within twenty-four hours of the meeting. And not by e-mail or voice mail but either live in person or on the phone, thus giving employees a chance to ask questions for clarification.

Even the most passive executives will call out their concerns about a decision if they know they'll be expected to go out and communicate it publicly. Of course, this assumes that if they don't communicate decisions to their people, the leader of the team will hold them accountable. Which is a great set-up for the next dysfunction.

But before we go there, let's look at another example of failure to gain commitment.

Lack of Buy-In Story

A pharmaceutical company I worked with was experiencing some profitability challenges and decided to cut costs. During an executive staff meeting, the CEO announced a proposal to eliminate business and first class air travel for all employees. I was amazed and, at the time, impressed by the support from the other executives, many of whom logged thousands and thousands of air miles each year.

Well, I later learned that only half the team went to their staff members and told them about the new rule. The others just decided to ignore it. You can imagine the problems this caused: employees from different organizations getting on a transatlantic flight, some going merrily to the front of the plane, others slogging toward the back. Beyond the anger and frustration that this caused, the hit to executive credibility was undeniable.

Could this have been a result of the team's proceeding without commitment clarification and cascading communication? In theory, yes. But in this particular case, as in so many, it came down to the unwillingness of those executive team members to stand up at the meeting and say, "This is really a terrible decision, and I don't like it."

Which brings us back to conflict, because the only way for those executives to buy in to a difficult decision like that would have been for the CEO to demand honest, unfiltered debate. But that didn't happen because that particular group of executives had little or no trust.

But now I'm moving backward within the model. Let's return to commitment.

Committing to Key Principles

The examples I've provided thus far speak to relatively tactical issues. When it comes to commitment, the most critical issues that team members must align themselves around are more enduring. Certainly, this includes behavioral norms, which include but are not

limited to conflict. Teams must commit to rules of engagement around timeliness at meetings, responsiveness in communication, and general interpersonal behavior.

But beyond behavioral commitment, there is the commitment to other principles such as purpose, values, mission, strategy, and goals. For more information about commitment to these principles, consult the book, *The Four Obsessions of an Extraordinary Executive,* which happens to be written by me.

Now, depending on the nature of your team and its role in your organization, some of these principles will be more important than others. However, I've found that every team, regardless of its size or level, must be able to commit to common goals.

Thematic Goals

At any given time, all the members of a team should know what its top collective priority is, and how they each contribute to addressing it. Achieving commitment around this is critical.

Perhaps the best way to do this, and to provoke team members to rally around a common cause, is to help them establish something I call a "thematic goal." This is nothing more than a single common unifying goal for the team, something that everyone on the team should be thinking about and working toward in the course of their daily responsibilities.

The Thematic Goal Story

I once worked with the executive team of a transportation company that had formed after a number of acquisitions of smaller firms over the prior two years. At the off-site meeting that I attended, the group determined that its thematic goal was to create a single company and work as one unit.

That didn't mean that each division and each functional team would stop performing its duties. Sales would continue to sell; Marketing would continue to market; Operations would continue to run operations. But what it did mean was that all the team members would go about their own responsibilities in a way that contributed to the achievement of creating a single, unified organization.

But the team members didn't stop there. They then identified the supporting objectives that would need to be accomplished for the team to say it had achieved the thematic goal:

- *Unifying the executive team*
- *Creating consistent business practices and policies*
- *Rationalizing different computer systems*
- *Creating a single brand and marketing message*
- *Establishing one approach to customer service and support*

Only after establishing this thematic goal and the supporting objectives did the team begin to create metrics around each of these areas. This would later serve as part of the team's scoreboard for measuring progress during weekly team meetings.

What is key here is that the team didn't start by committing to a set of metrics, but instead it created a context for those metrics.

The members also didn't divide up responsibility for each of the supporting objectives according to everyone's titles, they took collective ownership for them. This sense of common cause and unification often has a powerful effect on everyone in an organization if the leadership team effectively cascades that message and demonstrates commitment to it.

Now, at some point in the not-too-distant future (three months, six months, maybe a year) it will be time for the team to establish a new thematic goal. This will depend on a team's business cycle and the nature of change in a given industry.

KEY POINTS—ACHIEVING COMMITMENT

- Commitment requires clarity and buy-in.
- Clarity requires that teams avoid assumptions and ambiguity, and that they end discussions with a clear understanding about what they've decided upon.
- Buy-in does not require consensus. Members of great teams learn to disagree with one another and still commit to a decision.

OVERCOMING DYSFUNCTION #4

EMBRACING ACCOUNTABILITY

Accountability. It's a word that has become so overused, and misused, within the halls of many companies that it has lost much of its power. When it comes to teamwork, I define accountability as the willingness of team members to remind one another when they are not living up to the performance standards of the group.

The key to this kind of accountability is that it shouldn't always require the participation of the team leader. It is direct, peer-to-peer accountability, and it is based on the notion that peer pressure and the distaste for letting down a colleague will motivate a team player more than any fear of authoritative punishment or rebuke.

Peer pressure and the distaste for letting down a colleague will motivate a team player more than any fear of authoritative punishment or rebuke.

Ironically, for peer-to-peer accountability to become a part of a team's culture, it has to be modeled by the leader.

That's right. Even though I said earlier that the best kind of accountability is peer-to-peer, the key to making it stick is the willingness of the team leader to do something I call "enter the danger" whenever someone needs to be called on their behavior or performance. That means being willing to step right into the middle of a difficult issue and remind individual team members of their responsibility, both in terms of behavior and results.

But most leaders I know have a far easier time holding people accountable for their results than they do for behavioral issues. This is a problem because behavioral problems almost always precede results. That means team members have to be willing to call each other on behavioral issues, as uncomfortable as that might be, and if they see their leader balk at doing this, then they aren't going to do it themselves.

I've found that senior executives at large companies are some of the most egregious violators when it comes to failing to hold people accountable for behaviors, large or small.

The Lack of Accountability Story

One particular CEO I worked with could not bring himself to confront one of his staff members who was publicly and unapologetically criticizing the leadership development program that the CEO himself was sponsoring. "That's just how he is," was his response to a request to confront the problem. Another chief executive claimed "I don't have the time or energy for that" when someone suggested that he tell one of his direct reports to stop spreading unfounded rumors about his own promotion to president of the company.

Neither of these two CEOs would be considered wimpy; they wouldn't hesitate for too long to fire an executive who wasn't producing. However, like most of the CEOs I've worked with, they just didn't like the thought of having to tell someone that they needed to behave better.

Another Lack of Accountability Story

I once attended a staff meeting where one of the executives had his laptop open and was intermittently typing away during discussions. After the meeting I asked the CEO, "Does that bother you when he does that?" He told me, "Yeah, I find it distracting." So I asked the obvious question: "Why don't you tell him to stop?" A pained look came across the CEO's face as he answered, "I don't know. I'm not his parent. Who am I to tell him how to act . . ." I wanted to interrupt him and scream, "You're the friggin' CEO! That's who you are!" But I didn't. That's because I too sometimes struggle with accountability.

Why are the team leader's actions so important when it comes to setting a tone? Because if the rest of the team knows that the leader will eventually step in and call someone on something, they won't feel like they're stepping over the line doing it themselves. "He's going to tell you eventually anyway, so I thought I might as well save you the time and trouble."

But if everyone knows the leader doesn't have the courage to hold people accountable for their behaviors, they're going to reason with themselves, "Why should I play the heavy? Besides, he'll probably just let them off the hook eventually anyway."

Finally, perhaps the most important challenge of building a team where people hold one another accountable is overcoming the understandable hesitance of human beings to give one another critical feedback. Sometimes the tightest teams are the most reluctant to do this, even when the feedback is clearly constructive, because they don't want to risk the positive emotional environment that exists, which they probably value greatly.

Of course, when teammates stop holding one another accountable, what ultimately happens over time is that they lose respect for each other, and those good feelings begin to fade. Still, human beings often choose a path of slow, uncomfortable decline rather than risk a dramatic drop in morale caused by an ugly incident.

The most important challenge of building a team where people hold one another accountable is overcoming the understandable hesitance of human beings to give one another critical feedback.

I've found that the most effective way to overcome this hesitance is to help people realize that when they fail to provide peers with constructive feedback they are letting them down personally. By holding back, we are hurting not only the team, but also our teammates themselves. Sometimes this is the only compelling argument that can convince a well-meaning and caring teammate to step into the discomfort of telling someone what they need to hear. I know it works for me.

TOOLS AND EXERCISES

Team Effectiveness Exercise

One of the best ways I've found to encourage a culture of peer-to-peer accountability on a team is a simple tool my colleagues and I call the Team Effectiveness Exercise (TEE). Before explaining the mechanics of the TEE, let me make it clear that this is an exercise for teams that have already built some trust, and that have worked together long enough (two or three months, at the least) to have formed observation-based opinions of one another.

We use the TEE with almost every executive team we work with, and it's one of my favorite parts of the consulting we do. That's because it is both quick and amazingly effective. Here's how it works.

During an off-site meeting, or any other session where you have well over an hour available, have everyone on the team write down their answers to two simple questions about every member of the team, excluding themselves. The first question: "What is the single most important behavioral characteristic or quality demonstrated by this person that contributes to the strength of our team?" The second: "What is the single most important behavioral characteristic or quality demonstrated by this person that can sometimes derail the team?"

Help people realize that when they fail to provide peers with constructive feedback they are letting them down personally. By holding back, we are hurting not only the team, but also our teammates themselves.

Once everyone has finished jotting down their answers, the facilitator starts by putting the leader of the team up first. One by one, the team members each read their positive quality of the leader. The leader cannot respond to any of the feedback, other than to ask for clarification if something isn't clear. When everyone has gone, the facilitator asks the leader for any general reaction. Surprised? Not surprised? In most cases, the answers from the team are remarkably consistent, not to mention graciously offered, and the leader (like everyone else) is amazed to realize that the team really does understand what he or she is good at and how it helps the team.

Then, the facilitator goes around the room (I like to go in the opposite direction) asking each member to provide their constructive feedback to the leader. Again, the responses are usually consistent and tactfully, graciously offered. And when everyone is finished, the leader again is asked for a general reaction. Usually, the response is, "Yep, those are definitely my areas for improvement. Can't argue with that." Or something of that nature.

And the room is often slightly dumbfounded because they've just given their leader more direct, honest, and unequivocal feedback than they've ever offered before.

Of course, now that the leader has served as a role model for the exercise, the rest of the team is up, one by one. This can take as long as two hours, but usually less.

By the time the exercise is over, two separate but related feelings fill the room. The team members, even the difficult ones, are genuinely flattered by the specific positive feedback they've received. And they're collectively amazed by the clarity and simplicity of what they all need to do to improve for the team to grow.

Pretty simple. Pretty daunting, at least initially. But for a variety of reasons, this exercise yields amazing and powerful results virtually every time we use it. Here's why:

- There is not enough time for people to sit and think about their answers and wonder, "What are they going to say about me?" It happens so fast that people almost never "game" the process. The honesty is astounding.

- Because the leader goes first, it's tough for anyone to be defensive. Of course, this means the leader *must* do a good job of receiving feedback, both negative and positive.
- Because people are asked for just *one* positive and *one* negative, there is a sense of focus and priority, unlike many formal 360-degree programs that provide the victim with a list of thirty-five key improvement areas.

Now it's important to follow up the TEE so that the benefits of it don't fade quickly. The first way to do this is to have all team members e-mail their areas of strength and areas for improvement to the team leader. Then, a few months after the session where the exercise took place, the team should review those areas and discuss them again. What's critical is that team members know that the areas that were identified will not go away, and that they will have to answer for their progress in the not-too-distant future.

What's critical is that team members know that the areas that were identified will not go away, and that they will have to answer for their progress in the not-too-distant future.

Meetings and Accountability

While a sense of accountability should pervade virtually every aspect of organizational life at a great company, the place where it must be demonstrated and addressed most clearly is meetings. And there are two important steps in making this happen.

First, team members must know what each of the others is working on in order to hold them accountable. The best way to do this is to do something I call the "lightning round" at the beginning of regular meetings. This entails asking team members to each take no more than thirty seconds to update the team about their three top priorities that week. If anyone on the team feels that a given team member is spending time unwisely, or that there is greater need for a person's time and energy in another area, this is the place to call the question. Of course, as always, this assumes a level of trust and openness to conflict, as well as an original commitment to the team's goals.

Second, and more important still, the team must track progress against its goals and highlight any shortcomings before they become problematic. A great way to identify those shortcomings is to keep the team focused on a scoreboard or radar screen where key goals (thematic goals and supporting categorical objectives) are tracked. I'll be explaining the concept of the scoreboard in the next section, which happens to be right now.

KEY POINTS—EMBRACING ACCOUNTABILITY

- ▲ **Accountability on a strong team occurs directly among peers.**
- ▲ **For a culture of accountability to thrive, a leader must demonstrate a willingness to confront difficult issues.**
- ▲ **The best opportunity for holding one another accountable occurs during meetings, and the regular review of a team scoreboard provides a clear context for doing so.**

OVERCOMING DYSFUNCTION #5

FOCUSING ON RESULTS

Okay, if team members trust one another, engage in healthy conflict around issues, commit to the decisions they make, and hold one another accountable for those decisions, there is a pretty good chance they're going to make it.

Unfortunately, when we build teams we rarely, if ever, go about it in a linear, chronological way. For instance, I don't wait until my clients have completely addressed all of the first four dysfunctions before moving on to the fifth.

But even if we could, even if a team had overcome each dysfunction and seemed on the verge of the teamwork hall of fame (there isn't one, by the way), there would still be a chance that it would stumble and lose sight of the ultimate measure of a great team: results. And that's because your team is made up of extremely fallible human beings.

What is it about us that makes it so hard to stay focused on results? It's this thing called self-interest. And self-preservation. We have a strong and natural tendency to look out for ourselves before others, even when those others are part of our families and our teams.

We have a strong and natural tendency to look out for ourselves before others, even when those others are part of our families and our teams.

And once that tendency kicks in on a team, it can spread like a disease, quickly eroding the roots of teamwork until eventually even trust has been destroyed.

How do we avoid this? The key lies in keeping results in the forefront of people's minds. There is a reason that old saying "out of sight, out of mind" is used so often: it's true! A good way to focus attention is to use a visible scoreboard of some kind. Why a scoreboard?

Consider a football team. On a football field, a scoreboard focuses everyone's efforts on one thing: winning. It doesn't display defensive statistics or offensive statistics or individual player statistics. It provides unambiguous information about how the team is doing, and how much time the members have left if they want to improve the final outcome. That leaves little room for individual interpretation.

Teams have to eliminate ambiguity and interpretation when it comes to success.

Imagine the quarterback of a team that is losing by fourteen points with three minutes to go in the game saying to the coach, "Well, I feel pretty good about things. I mean, my performance was not bad, and my stats look good." The coach would be furious. He wants that quarterback, and everyone else on the team, to be focused on one thing: winning. And the only thing a team has to do to know whether it's winning is to look at the scoreboard.

Teams within organizations need to do the same thing. They have to eliminate ambiguity and interpretation when it comes to success. It's ironic that so many teams don't do this, because they have an advantage over sports teams: they often get to create their own scoreboard! They decide what it is they want to achieve, and how they want to measure their success.

Certainly, many large and public companies don't have the same kind of luxury, because they're accountable for quarterly numbers and a stock price. But even those companies, and certainly the smaller ones, get to decide how they want to go about running their businesses. And even within large, public companies, the departmental teams that make up the company have a say in what they do. And that means they construct their own scoreboards, which I'll describe further on page 79.

But should they measure their team's success in terms of market share? Client satisfaction? Pure revenue? Profit? Growth over last year? Growth versus competitors? Versus the industry average? Key milestones? There are only two consistently *wrong* answers: *none of the above* and *all of them.* Pick one. Or maybe two. But by all means, pick something so that team members have something they can collectively focus upon and around which they can rally. (See page 136 for a more detailed description of thematic goals.)

Far too many teams assess their success using subjective and unreliable means like politics ("Is the CEO happy with us this month?"), feelings ("I *feel* like we're doing pretty well right now"), or outside opinion ("Did you see what that analyst wrote about us in his industry report?")—but none of this really matters.

Results-oriented teams establish their own measurements for success. They don't allow themselves the wiggle room of subjectivity. But this is not easy, because subjectivity is attractive.

Results-oriented teams establish their own measurements for success. They don't allow themselves the wiggle room of subjectivity. But this is not easy, because subjectivity is attractive.

I know how easy it is to fall into this trap, because I do it myself. I don't like to be limited in how I measure my success to a few numbers that might not tell the whole story. But I know that this is just an excuse, or better yet, a manifestation of my desire to change my mind and reinterpret my success based on what's going on at a given point in time. Ultimately, ambiguity and loose interpretation catch up to you, usually in the form of the bottom line.

So how does a team avoid this pitfall? By committing, early and publicly, to what it will achieve, and by constantly reviewing its progress against those expected achievements (a.k.a. the scoreboard). If it's a regular meeting where the key metrics are reviewed and discussed, great. If it's an online scoreboard where every major goal is tracked, terrific. If that's a piece of butcher paper on the wall with the updated numbers, good enough.

When players on a team stop caring about the scoreboard, they inevitably start caring about something else.

But remember, this isn't about measuring *everything*. That creates just as much confusion by overwhelming people. This is about giving people a simple way to gauge their success and to stay focused on the right priorities so that they aren't distracted by something else.

Distractions

What might that something else be? How about their individual career advancement? Or their compensation? Or their ego? Their standing within the department? When players on a team stop caring about the scoreboard, they inevitably start caring about something else. And that something else is usually not the team.

The Individual Over the Team Story

Years ago, when basketball superstar Michael Jordan retired (for the first time) from the Chicago Bulls, a great player, Scottie Pippen, became the leader of the team. Even without Jordan, the Bulls were considered one of the best teams in the league, and had just as much chance to win the championship as anyone else.

During the playoffs that year, the Bulls were tied with their rival, the New York Knicks, with just a few seconds to go in the game. The coach of the Bulls called time out and drew up a set play for his team to take the final shot of the game. His play called for that shot to be taken by a player other than Pippen.

Disappointed that he wouldn't be playing the key role in deciding the game, Pippen refused to go out on the court for the last few seconds. Fans and announcers, not to mention the players themselves, were dumbfounded. In essence, Pippen was announcing to the world—and certainly to his teammates—that the collective results of the team were not as important as his own stardom.

The Bulls made their shot and won the game. And to his credit, Pippen went into the locker room after the game and took his lumps from his teammates, later admitting that what he had done was wrong.

And just in case we're tempted to believe that this would never happen in a corporate environment, consider the following examples.

The Second Individual Over the Team Story

A client's products were growing obsolete, and the CEO announced to his team that they would need to focus on innovation in order to prevent an imminent revenue problem. The chief scientist of the company, whose job it was to run research and development, seemed less than enthusiastic about the charge. When pressed, he finally admitted, "I don't get paid enough to innovate. I want to get paid royalties for what I invent."

Yet Another Individual Over the Team Story

Another client, this one a start-up, had just hired its final executive team member, a highly sought-after chief technology officer. When the CEO indicated that everyone in the company should be willing to do whatever was necessary to make the company fly, "including sweep the floors," the CTO replied, "I don't have near enough stock to sweep floors."

In both of these situations, the difficult executives quickly left their teams.

The point of these stories is that human beings are naturally self-interested. Only by ensuring that the people on your team are committed to collective results ahead of their own needs, and by keeping them focused on those results, can you avoid the kind of individualization that breaks teams apart.

Because these self-oriented distractions are such powerful destroyers of teams, it is worthwhile to look at and understand them all.

Distraction #1: Ego

Ego is the ultimate killer on a team, and it is an insidious one. That's because it lurks deep in the heart of every team member. As much as we want our teams to win, at a basic level we want to win as individuals first.

As a kid, I remember playing on some bad Little League teams, but making the all-star team. If you had asked me then if I would have traded my all-star status for a few extra wins, I'd probably have said "no way."

As an adult, I've been fortunate to learn to enjoy the collective benefits of team accomplishments more than individual ones, but there is always that little voice in your head saying, "What about me?" Sometimes that little voice drowns out the cry of the team, and the collective results of the group get left behind.

There is always that little voice in your head saying, "What about me?" Sometimes that little voice drowns out the cry of the team, and the collective results of the group get left behind.

I've worked with many executive teams that were failing as a group, but somehow, the majority of the people on the team seemed to be in good spirits. Looking under the covers, I discovered that only the individuals who were failing were unhappy. It was as though the others were saying, "Well, at least *my* area is doing well."

This is probably one of the top two or three things that separate good teams from bad ones. On strong teams, no one is happy until everyone is succeeding, because that's the only way to achieve the collective results of the group. Of course, this implies that individual egos are less important than team achievements.

Distractions #2 and #3: Career Development and Money

Even the most altruistic team members will at times have to focus on their own career advancement and financial needs. After all, they have families, mortgages, and tuition payments to think about.

A great team will understand those needs, and the validity of them, but not let them distract the team from achieving the collective goals. The key to doing that is being open about what people need, and not making them feel guilty or selfish for acknowledging those needs. That might sound unrealistic, but remember, if team members trust one another, then they're willing to be vulnerable. And admitting that you're uncomfortable with your career advancement or salary or anything else that is personal is nothing if not a statement of vulnerability. If there is trust among team members, no one will take the comment as selfish or anti-team. In fact, they should be glad that the person put the issue on the table for everyone to help with, because if they don't, then it will eventually fester and create problems that impact the team's performance.

And after all, the performance of the team is what matters. Anything that stands in the way of performance must be addressed openly and directly, even if it is something that is sensitive to one or more members of the team.

Distraction #4: My Department

This is perhaps the most subtle and dangerous distraction of all because well-intentioned team members often succumb to it, and because they actually wear it as a badge of honor. The departmental distraction is the tendency of team members to place a higher priority on the team they lead than they place on the team they are a member of. I call this the "Team #1 Dilemma."

The Team #1 Dilemma

Give a group of team members some truth serum and ask them which is their first priority—the team they manage or the team they're a member of—and many of them will admit that it is the team they lead. And when you think about it, this makes sense.

After all, they probably hired (a.k.a. picked) the people on their team. They might very well spend more time with them. As a result, they will probably like their own team more. They probably feel a sense of responsibility for their team, and convince themselves that their people would feel betrayed or abandoned if their leader felt a slightly stronger allegiance to the team above than to the one below.

In reality, employees want their leaders to be strong team members on the teams above. They know that they ultimately pay the price when their manager doesn't get along with or cooperate with managers of other departments, leaving the staff to navigate the treacherous and bloody waters of organizational politics.

Employees know that they ultimately pay the price when their manager doesn't get along with or cooperate with managers of other departments, leaving the staff to navigate the treacherous and bloody waters of organizational politics.

In truth, many leaders who choose the teams they lead over the ones they belong to are doing so because they like being leaders more than they like being followers.

As understandable as this is, it is a recipe for team disaster. When members of a team fail to make that team more important than their own teams, they create something I like to call the "United Nations Syndrome." Or you can call it the "Congressional Syndrome." Rather than coming together to make the best possible decision for the entire organization, they become lobbyers for their own constituents. In essence, whenever push comes to shove, they compete with their teammates rather than collaborate with them.

Now this is usually okay for the United Nations or Congress, groups that are explicitly not teams. The founding fathers of the United States, for instance, recognized what they called "self-interest rightly understood" and created a government that respected it and provided a sense of balance. (Okay, that's the end of today's civics lesson.)

The key to success for a team is that its members go beyond barter and compromise to embrace a collective pursuit of the best interests of the whole.

A team, however, is a different kind of institution. The key to success for a team is that its members go beyond barter and compromise to embrace a collective pursuit of the best interests of the whole. Like a family, they make sacrifices for one another with the only expectation of repayment being greater team success.

They offer up their own headcount, budget, accolades, and prestige without hesitation or complaint. Why? Because their sense of self-esteem and achievement is not individual but rather collective.

If you stop and think about that for a moment, it is pretty powerful. How does a group of people who are more interested in their own individual needs compete against such a team? They usually lose.

TOOLS AND EXERCISES

Scoreboard

There is one simple method for ensuring that a team doesn't lose sight of results: the scoreboard. Some teams may call this a dashboard, a radar screen, or even just a list of metrics. In any case, every team should have a single, easy-to-read visual tool for assessing its success at any given point in time.

The components of that scoreboard will vary depending on the size and scope of a team, not to mention the industry. However, a good scoreboard will be limited to a relatively small number of critical factors. And while it will be largely quantitative (revenue, expenses, schedules, and so on), it should incorporate an element of qualitative assessment on the part of the team.

The best way to create a scoreboard is to draw upon two primary sources: the ongoing metrics of the team (again, revenue, expenses, schedules, customer service numbers, and the like) and the supporting objectives, which form the team's thematic goal.

Aside from the creation and publication of a team scoreboard, there is no real activity or tool for ensuring results. The best tools and exercises for doing this are the ones that ensure trust, conflict, commitment, and accountability, because these will ultimately pave the way for team success.

KEY POINTS—FOCUSING ON RESULTS

- ▲ The true measure of a great team is that it accomplishes the results it sets out to achieve.
- ▲ To avoid distractions, team members must prioritize the results of the team over their individual or departmental needs.
- ▲ To stay focused, teams must publicly clarify their desired results and keep them visible.

SECTION THREE

Answering Questions and Anticipating Problems

My colleagues and I receive plenty of good questions all the time from clients, consultants, executives, and managers. And we've had to address various objections and obstacles with our clients before and during team-building sessions. So I thought, "Hey, let's put all that stuff in the book too."

COMMON QUESTIONS

How long does it take to build a team?

Our research indicates that in North America, it takes thirty-nine days. In Europe and Asia, thirty-eight.

I'm kidding. It's impossible to answer this question for a variety of reasons, not the least of which is "Does a team ever really complete the process?" It's more of an ongoing process, like a marriage.

Another reason why it's tough to answer is that so many factors influence a team's progress. I'll list them here in the form of questions, like *Jeopardy:*

- How much time has been set aside for team building?
- How committed are the members to becoming a team?
- How many members are there?
- Are they all located in the same city or office?
- How much history does the group already have?
- Is that history positive or negative?
- How strong and credible is the leader?

Okay, now that I've sufficiently qualified my answer, let me say that if I were forced to provide a concrete time frame, on average I would say that a new team can make substantial progress in two or three months. That assumes that the team members have one or two off-site meetings during that span, and that they regularly spend time together during meetings and various working sessions.

Having said all that, a team can actually make dramatic progress in far less time. Even a few days.

How many people should be on a team?

This is the $64,000 question, for sure. And while there is no way to answer it definitively for every organization, I believe the range is from three to twelve.

Most organizations I work with err on the side of including too many people on a team, in many cases because they don't want to exclude anyone. It's as though they're mistakenly viewing team membership as a reward or a benefit rather than as a strategic decision about how to best run the organization. And while I salute the desire to be inclusive, there are some big problems with having too many people on a team:

- On a purely practical and tactical note, it's tough to coordinate meetings and other team activities when there are fifteen schedules to consider.
- More important, it's difficult for team members to get to know one another, develop bonds of trust with one another, when there are too many people in the room. Generally speaking, a kid who grows up in a family of ten children is probably not going to have as deep and meaningful relationship with most siblings as a kid born to a family of four. Generally speaking, that is.

- But perhaps most important of all, having too many people on a team makes team dynamics during meetings and other decision-making events almost impossible. That's because a good team has to engage in two types of communication in order to optimize decision making, but only one of these is practical in a large group.

  According to Harvard's Chris Argyris, those two types of communication are advocacy and inquiry. Basically, *advocacy* is the statement of ideas and opinions; *inquiry* is the asking of questions for clarity and understanding. When a group gets too large, people realize they are not going to get the floor back any time soon, so they resort almost exclusively to advocacy. It becomes like Congress (which is *not* designed to be a team) or the United Nations (ditto).

  One member says, "I think we should pursue proposal A," provoking another member to say, "Well, I think we should pursue proposal B." Someone else lobbies for C, yet another person wants A with a slight modification, and before you know it, everyone is trying to get their opinion heard.

  Inquiry, on the other hand, would entail one of the members saying, "Wait a minute. I'd like to hear you explain why you support proposal A, because I want to understand your rationale. After all, if it makes sense, I could go along with it." Okay, that might be just a little too idealistic, but you get the point.

How likely is it that you'll have to lose (remove) a member of the team in order to make progress?

This is a tough question, but an important one. First, let me be clear: getting rid of someone on the team is *not* a standard part of our team-building process. Ironically, however, being *willing* to lose a team member will greatly decrease the likelihood that you'll have to do so. How can that be?

Because if everyone on the team knows that the leader is willing to remove someone if doing so is in the best collective interest of the group, then they will be far more likely to consider behavioral change. This, in turn, increases the likelihood that no one will actually need to be removed.

On the other hand, if everyone knows that the leader is unwilling to even consider swapping out a difficult team member, they'll be more likely to dig in their heels and resist change. It actually makes sense, doesn't it?

Now, I'd be naive if I didn't admit that there are times when one member of a team, or more, needs to be replaced in order for the team to gel. It shows up in sports, business, classrooms, and every other team dynamic.

However, I would say that most of the teams we work with don't find it necessary to replace a member during the six months after embarking on a team-improvement process. I'd also say that many of them do after a period of six months to a year as the team evolves and grows, sometimes beyond the interest or capability of a given member.

How much can be accomplished during a two-day off-site session?

Short answer: a lot. I've seen new teams establish nontrivial bonds that last for years in just one session. And I've seen dysfunctional teams address painful issues that have plagued them for years over the course of a day and a half.

But here's the thing: that kind of progress is often a little painful. And exhausting. It requires good old-fashioned hard work.

Remember, good team-building off-sites are not boondoggles—excuses for golfing and massages. And they're not about catching each other falling off a chair or climbing a tree. They're intense, focused, and grounded in operational issues, not touchy-feely ones. If a team goes away for a two-day off-site and spends six hours riding bicycles and playing bocce ball, its members aren't going to get two full days of benefit out of the experience.

If I'm a manager of the team, should I use an outside consultant or facilitator?

The key to this question is whether you can find a really good consultant or facilitator. If not, then go it alone. If you know of someone who is practical, trustworthy, and skillful, then it might be a good idea to bring them in.

The benefit of having an outsider help you is that you can take part in the process as a member of the team—which you are—rather than having to also play the role of facilitator. Now, some managers and executives are quite good at this; others are not. So, like so many other things in life, it really depends.

For those who are reluctant to spend money on an outsider, it's important to consider the hidden but staggering costs associated with being a dysfunctional team. The cost of losing and having to replace one good team member will more than cover any initial expense for a good consultant. And that's before factoring in the value of higher productivity and reduced stress.

OBJECTIONS FROM PARTICIPANTS

"We can't take two whole days out of the office!"

The most precious commodity for any team, executive or otherwise, is time. Not money. And so the most common, and frankly, most effective objection that we hear from leaders and team members is "There is no way we can afford to spend two full days out of the office!"

Of course, this is either a miscalculation of the cost-benefit relationship associated with teamwork or, just as likely, a body-blow attempt to prevent a team-building initiative from getting started at all.

Whether you're a leader or a consultant, be prepared for this objection, and if at all possible, eliminate it by beating the proponent to the punch.

Explain up front—before the initiative begins—how much time is already being wasted because of politics, confusion, internal competition, and revisiting issues over and over again. Sell the program like you would any other product or service, by illustrating the problems that exist and proposing a practical solution. Take the "we don't have time" issue off the table before anyone can raise it.

"But we have real work to do!"

This is a continuation of the first objection, but with a different spin. Again, you want to respond to this one with confidence: building a team *is* real work because it is all about getting more work done in less time. If people want to measure productivity in terms of forty-eight-hour increments, then I suppose that leaving the office for two days might set a team back a few hours in terms of time away from e-mail and voice mail and whatever individual contributor jobs people have.

But when measured in a more reasonable time frame—a year, six months, three months, heck, even two weeks—the productivity achieved by focusing on working as a team easily outweighs a day or two away from the office.

Adrenaline Addiction

All of this highlights one of the most challenging obstacles that prevents teams from taking the time to work on how they work together: adrenaline addiction. Many if not most of the executives and managers I know have become so hooked on the rush of urgent demands and out-of-control schedules that the prospect of slowing down to review, think, talk, and develop themselves is too anxiety-inducing to consider. Of course, this is exactly what they need, which is what addiction is all about—doing things that are bad for you even when confronted with evidence that they are, well, bad for you.

One suggestion: call it what it is. Confront people with the idea that they may be victims of an adrenaline addiction. There is something about describing it that way that makes people sit back and listen. At least for a few minutes—until the need for a rush hits them again. But maybe those few minutes are what you need to get them to commit to building the team.

"These touchy-feely sessions are nonsense!"

The best way to deal with this objection is to agree. Because I certainly do. Touchy-feely sessions *are* nonsense. But that is not what this book, and the programs we're describing, are all about.

They're about getting more done in less time. They're about making better decisions, faster. They're about keeping your best performers, and possibly helping the poorer ones to improve—or find another place to work. And they're about achieving results.

There is nothing touchy-feely about this. Just because some consultants and authors have taken a touchy-feely, new-age approach to team building doesn't mean that what you're proposing isn't practical. Because it has to be practical.

As the leader or facilitator, it is your responsibility to ensure that you are grounding the team-building process within the practical and tactical realities of the business of the team. And it is your responsibility to handle, even welcome, these kinds of objections as an opportunity to establish the practical tone of your team-building effort.

So the best way to deal with this concern is to address it head on. "I hate touchy-feely sessions too, and that's why this isn't going to be one of those. We aren't going to be catching one another falling off of a chair. And we're not going to be getting naked, holding hands, or singing songs . . ."

"This is just another flavor of the month. Next quarter we'll be on to something new."

The key to answering this objection is to prove it false. The leader of a team, more than the facilitator, must make it clear to the team that this is not going to go away, that there is nowhere to run, nowhere to hide. Of course, then the leader must not allow anyone to run away and hide.

Even if the fear of losing momentum coming out of the off-site isn't enough to scare a leader, the prospect of losing credibility should be.

So, as I asked at the beginning of this book, before embarking on this process, leaders must ask themselves if they're willing and able to follow through.

OBSTACLES TO AVOID

The leader isn't truly committed to building a team.

This is another tough one. The fact is, leadership matters. If the leader of a team doesn't understand the power of teamwork and isn't prepared to lead the effort in terms of setting an example and dedicating time to it, then the chances of success are basically zero.

However, many leaders who might seem uninterested in teamwork are often just skeptical about the possibility of achieving it, or are afraid that acknowledging the need for it might reflect poorly on them. In these cases, success is possible, as long as they're willing to start the process with good intentions.

We've worked with many skeptical—not cynical, but skeptical—leaders who have changed their attitude about building their team after just a few hours. When they realize that building a team is not a touchy-feely group grope but rather an attempt to improve the business, they begin to warm up to the idea. And when they discover that their staff members really do want to work hard, and that they're actually rooting for the leader to succeed, the sky's the limit. (Well, that might be a bit of an overstatement, but I got caught up in the moment.)

One way to help leaders overcome their initial doubts and understand the real nature of team building is to let them read *The Five Dysfunctions* book. I realize that this might sound self-serving—

and I suppose it is—but the power of the story is that it allows readers to detach from the lessons by getting caught up in the characters. Before they know what's hit them, they're thinking about themselves and how they can accomplish what Kathryn, the main character in the book, has accomplished.

If this doesn't work, you might want to consider anonymously sending a copy of the book to your leader every day for a year. Just a thought.

Team members are holding back.

Sometimes people decide not to oppose a team-building effort actively but rather to sit back and derail the effort passively. And to be fair, sometimes people do this without malice, just because they're uncomfortable. In any case, know that this is not only an easily addressed issue, it is a hidden opportunity for a radical conversion. But the only way that I've found to win converts among the skeptics is to face them head on.

That's right. As initially awkward as it is to confront someone ("Fred, it seems like you're not engaging here. Are you uncomfortable with what we're doing, or is there another issue you want to help us understand?"), it is often the most effective way to defuse tension in the room and move the team forward.

And think about it this way. When a difficult team member decides to hold back and passively resist the team-building effort, the goal is to make others in the room uncomfortable enough to back off. That is victory for the resistant member—when the leader blinks. It's like a game of chicken, and your opponent wants you to bail out first.

So I guess the lesson here is this: team leaders or consultants can only overcome resistance among team members by overcoming their own resistance or fear of discomfort first.

Someone is dominating the session.

Instead of holding back, sometimes team members can do the opposite—they dominate the conversation. Dealing with this is a little trickier than it might seem, but nonetheless, it is doable.

First, understanding the motivation for dominating is key. Is the person just a naturally talkative, conversation-dominating kind of person? If so, then the team is probably used to it, which calls on the team leader or consultant to take an appropriately gentle approach.

And this is another area where the Myers-Briggs or some other profiling tool can come in handy. ("Okay, Fred. As an extrovert, you're comfortable speaking up quickly and thinking out loud. Which is fine. But we need you to help draw out the others on the team who might not be as open with their ideas . . .") Whatever.

In most of these situations, well-intentioned team members will quickly and gladly edit their behavior. Of course, fifteen minutes later they'll need to be gently reminded again, but they'll be okay with that.

But if the dominating person has another agenda, perhaps one driven by insecurity or the need to manipulate the session, a more direct approach may be necessary. Now, I'm not talking about a serial killer here, or even a psychologically unbalanced team member. I'm thinking more along the lines of a person who *really* doesn't want to be vulnerable, and who tries to control the dynamics in the room to avoid it.

Thankfully, the exercises outlined in this book often provide exactly the right kind of opportunity to help that person get comfortable. But from time to time, a facilitator will have to confront people to help them admit what their concerns are. This might need to happen during a break, one on one, if the situation seems particularly difficult.

And ultimately, if the exercises and gentle prodding of the facilitator don't bring about the desired improvement, it might be time to start thinking about whether that person is capable of being a productive member of the team. But that's only for when the other methods have truly been exhausted.

Team members are geographically dispersed and don't spend much time together.

There should be no doubt about the fact that having all members of a team in one location is a distinct advantage. People must spend time together to develop trust, learn to engage in conflict, and do all of the other things that are signs of real teamwork. Physical separation makes that difficult.

But not impossible. Many teams must rely on phones, videoconferencing, and other forms of technology to interact, and some of these methods are remarkably effective.

However, for some activities, there is simply no substitute for face-to-face interaction. What kind of activities am I referring to? Team-building activity, for one. And major discussions of strategy.

No matter how advanced videoconferencing becomes (and it has a long way to go), it is just not realistic to expect people to be emotionally vulnerable, provide constructive feedback, and hold one another accountable for their behaviors over a T1 line. There is something uniquely powerful about being in a room together, and being able to read the body language, facial expressions, and other subtle behavioral cues.

All of this means that people must commit to getting together on a regular basis—monthly, maybe quarterly—and using that time effectively, if they are going to become a team. Unfortunately, too many teams use their scarce time together primarily for social activities. And while there is certainly a place and a need for social interaction among team members, it should not occur at the expense of substantive team building and problem solving.

A top performer isn't interested in or committed to the team-building process.

This is a classic challenge for teams and their leaders, and a difficult one. But the answer is clear. Great teams are made up of great team members. And as painful as it is in the short term—and it is certainly painful—a team is better off removing a talented but disruptive team member for the long-term good of the team. Professional sports are littered with examples of teams that lose their star player only to improve their team performance the next year and beyond.

Of course, this is easier said than done, especially when you're staring at a monthly report and your disruptive team member is at the top of the list and bringing in 45 percent of your revenue.

The key to developing the courage to take action comes from understanding the hidden impact on the other members of a team that results from allowing the disruptive employee to continue without consequences. By not taking action, a leader is actually condoning the action of that employee, and confusing others in the department. Oftentimes, when a leader finally removes that member, the performance of the others increases almost immediately.

Having said all this, I want to be clear about one thing: before you take aim at your top performers, make sure that they are not capable of being turned around. Some people have never been held accountable for being a strong team member, and simply need a leader to show them the way. Moving too fast before doing due diligence is not wise. Shooting yourself in the foot to make a point is never a good idea.

A team member reports to two different teams.

In many matrixed organizations, this poses a difficult problem. The answer lies in the removal of ambiguity and in addressing the situation head on.

For instance, when a team member has responsibility to two teams, the question that must be asked is: Which team takes precedence? Because one of them has to be more important than the other. That is not to say that the person can't serve both, but when push comes to shove—and it will at some point—it will be best if everyone knows where that person's primary allegiance falls. There is nothing politically incorrect about this. It is simply a matter of being clear.

Now, the people who must ultimately decide which of the two teams wins out in the event of a conflict are the leaders of those teams. Only they, or someone higher in the organization, can make that call. Certainly, it should not be the torn team member, although too often that is the unfortunate case.

SECTION FOUR

Building the Team

This section provides a host of exercises, schedules, definitions, and references so that you can create a team-building process that best suits your organization.

▲

TEAM-BUILDING ROAD MAP

This segment provides a framework for a comprehensive team-building process over a six-month period. Some teams may want to use a more aggressive time line, while others may take a slower approach. In any case, the following is a general outline of the steps any team should be prepared to take.

Warning: There is one big point I want to make here, and it is critical:

DON'T DO EVERYTHING EXACTLY THE WAY IT IS DESCRIBED HERE!

The purpose of this field guide, and this section in particular, is to give you as much framework and structure as you need to make your team better, not to prescribe or dictate a detailed agenda.

I've provided detail not to limit your freedom of judgment but to give you as much information as you might need to fully understand how these ideas can be implemented. However, as in all important undertakings, judgment and flexibility are key.

TIME LINE

Week 1: Preliminary Work for the Initial Off-Site

Before the initial off-site takes place, team members will have to spend approximately one hour completing two assessments:

- Five Dysfunctions Team Assessment (available on page 116) or a more comprehensive online version available at www.tablegroup.com. (There is a charge for the online version; however, it provides much richer analysis of team strengths and weaknesses.)

- Behavioral Profile Assessment (such as Myers-Briggs). We strongly recommend that teams do these assessments ahead of time to ensure that the time spent during the off-site is as focused and productive as possible. And because the advance work is extremely quick—even enjoyable—there is usually little if any resistance.

Week 2: Initial Off-Site

This is the one-and-a-half to two-day session that is the anchor of your team-building effort and the formal kickoff of your new approach to teamwork. It will include a review of your team's assessment, as well as various exercises around trust, conflict, commitment, accountability, and results. A comprehensive description of the initial off-site is provided in the next segment.

Off-Site Follow-Up

Immediately after the off-site ends, it is critical to distribute important notes to team members as a confirmation of the commitments they made, and for their ongoing reference and use during the months to follow.

Week 3: First Review Session

To maintain the momentum coming out of the initial off-site and avoid the lull that can sometimes occur, it is critical that teams meet and review the commitments they made the prior week. They should take a few minutes to review their behavioral and team profiles and tie up any loose ends that were left.

Weeks 4–12: Ongoing Reference and Discussion

During the weeks that follow the off-site and review session, team members should be referencing and discussing all relevant aspects of their team development process as they arise in the course of normal business activity. These will probably involve—but are not limited to—the team assessment, behavioral profiling, conflict profiles and norms, goal commitments, and team effectiveness development areas, as well as the team scoreboard.

Keep in mind that a *real* team should be spending considerable time together in meetings and working sessions. In fact, it is not uncommon that as much as 20 percent of each team member's time is spent working through issues and solving problems with the team as a whole.

Week 13: Quarterly Off-Site Review

This is a one- or two-day session during which team members review many of the assessments and profiles from the initial off-site, and more important, assess progress made by individuals and the team as a whole. Common activities would include a discussion of the level of productive conflict on the team, as well as a second pass at the Team Effectiveness Exercise. The first quarterly off-site review is a good opportunity to review progress made against the team's goals as well, as these are the best indication of real progress.

Weeks 14–25: Ongoing Reference and Discussion

During the next twelve weeks, team members should again be referencing and discussing relevant aspects of their team development process as they arise in the course of normal business activity. However, team members should now be more comfortable than before in holding one another accountable for any deviations from team norms and personal commitments.

Week 26: Final Off-Site Review

This is the last off-site within the context of the initial team-building effort, but certainly should not be the last such meeting for the team. During this session, team members should step back and assess progress made over the course of the past six months. This should include the reevaluation of the team using the same team assessment that was completed during Week 1. New areas for improvement should be identified and action plans for the future should be put in place.

Week 27 and Beyond

Like a marriage, a team is never completely finished developing itself. And so the team should be constantly addressing areas of deficiency, and it should be periodically stepping back to assess progress. And again, members of *real* teams spend considerable time working together.

THE INITIAL OFF-SITE

Another warning: The agenda that follows is not meant to prescribe or dictate how you build your team. It is simply a structure my colleagues and I have found to be useful with many of our clients. But keep in mind that every situation is a little different, and requires a measure of judgment, even art, on the part of the facilitator and leader.

So don't be afraid to deviate from this agenda—or from anything else in this guide, for that matter—to best serve the needs of your team and your unique situation.

Overview and Assessment (one or two hours)

Overview of the Five Dysfunctions (around half an hour)

Begin the off-site by providing the team with a clear and complete overview of the model; it is critical that everyone understands and embraces it. You can do this by presenting the model yourself and providing your own stories, or by showing The Table Group's video on *The Five Dysfunctions of a Team*. In either case, it is certainly helpful if team members have read *The Five Dysfunctions of a Team* ahead of time.

Review of Team Assessment Report Results (about one hour)

If the team completed the team assessment before the session, walk them through the results. If they have not, you can have them complete the short-form paper-based assessment shown on page 116 of this guide.

Once the team has reviewed—but certainly not resolved—the issues highlighted by the team report, you are ready to move on to the first part of team building: building trust.

Building Trust (two to four hours)

Personal Histories Exercise (around fifteen minutes)

The first step in building trust is helping people get comfortable being vulnerable with one another. (See page 118.)

Behavioral Profile Exercise (around two to four hours)

The next step in ensuring vulnerability-based trust is giving team members a tool for understanding themselves, and one another, in a deeper way. Behavioral profiling tools such as the Myers-Briggs make it easier for people to reveal their own strengths and weaknesses. (See page 119.)

Consider revisiting the findings from the Team Assessment Report that you reviewed at the beginning of the off-site. Often, a team's collective profile provides insights into why a team may or may not struggle with a particular dysfunction.

Trust Review

During a two-day off-site, the team should begin Day 2 by taking time to review team members' individual insights around their profiles and potential areas for improvement. (See Step 7 within Behavioral Profiling on page 120).

Mastering Conflict (one or two hours)

Conflict Profiling (around thirty to sixty minutes)

The next step in building your team is learning to engage in productive conflict around issues. To make this possible, it is important for the team to understand its collective and individual preferences for dealing with conflict. (See page 122.)

Your team may want to use other models, such as the Thomas-Kilmann Instrument and the Depth-Frequency Model to better assess its conflict profile. (See pages 129–131.)

Conflict Norming (around thirty minutes)

Once the team has determined its profile, it can then establish a set of norms around how the members will engage one another in conflict. (See page 123.)

Conflict Resolution Obstacles (around thirty to sixty minutes)

Even teams with clear norms around conflict can often struggle to resolve issues that they are debating because they encounter distractions unrelated to the issue being discussed. The Conflict Resolution Model can help them understand these distractions and eliminate them during conflict. (See page 124.)

Achieving Commitment (two to six hours)

Clarification of Team and Organizational Principles

This is the part of the off-site where the team begins diving into business-related topics.

Using the conflict norms and trust-related insights from the previous exercises, it is now time to clarify and commit to a variety of operational and behavioral principles, which may include core purpose, values, strategy, goals, roles, and team expectations around behavior.

Topics will vary depending on the nature of the team and its role in the organization (for example, executive leadership team, line management team, employee task force). All teams will want to clarify their thematic goals and supporting categorical objectives. (See page 134.)

Embracing Accountability (one or two hours)

Team Effectiveness Exercise

To create a culture of accountability, team members must learn to provide one another with direct feedback, both positive and constructive, around their behavior and performance. (See page 139.)

Focusing on Results (one hour)

Establishment of a Team Scoreboard

The team should create a means for quickly and effectively gauging its ongoing success against its goals. (See page 141.)

Off-Site Wrap-Up and Follow-Up

Commitment Clarification

To ensure alignment and clarity coming out of the off-site, the team must review what it has agreed upon and resulting actions that must be taken. (See page 132.)

Cascading Communication

To ensure consistent messaging, the team must be clear about when members are to communicate results of the off-site to their teams or others within the organization. (See page 133.)

Initial Off-Site Follow-Up

To ensure that momentum coming out of the off-site is not lost, it is important for team members to take specific steps to review, communicate, and follow up on the actions discussed and the commitments made. (See page 142.)

TOOLS AND EXERCISES IN DETAIL

This is the segment where we provide step-by-step instructions for using the tools and exercises mentioned in the earlier parts of the book.

PRELIMINARY WORK

Review of the Online Team Assessment

Purpose of exercise: To help the team identify its current strengths and weaknesses, and prepare them for the rest of the off-site.

Time required: One or two hours.

Instructions: This example assumes the team took the online version of the assessment and received their final team report, and thus has all the analysis that is included in it. Here is how to take them through that report:

1. Review the overall team profile and scores.
2. Ask the team to individually review the next three sections—Strengths, Areas for Improvement, and Areas of Key Difference—and look for particularly interesting highlights.
3. Have different team members read aloud the list of team strengths, areas for improvement, and areas of key differences.
4. Ask the group for their insight as to why the team scored the way it did, on all three areas. (You may also want to break the team up into smaller subgroups of three or four people and have them discuss why certain questions scored particularly high or low.)
5. Record their responses on flip charts for reference during the remainder of this session.
6. Clarify any misunderstandings or confusion that may arise around any particular question that has been highlighted.

PRELIMINARY WORK

Review of the Short-Form Team Assessment

Purpose of exercise: To help the team identify its predisposition to certain dysfunctions, and prepare them for the rest of the off-site.

Time required: Thirty to sixty minutes.

Instructions: This example assumes the team will fill out the assessment on the spot.

1. Hand out copies of the Team Assessment included on the following page, and give the team members time to complete it.
2. Ask team members to share their individual responses.
3. Average the team members' responses to determine the overall score for each dysfunction.
4. Ask the group for their insight as to why the team scored the way it did. (You may also want to break the team up into smaller subgroups of three or four people and have them discuss why certain questions scored particularly high or low.)
5. Record their responses on flip charts for reference during the remainder of this session.
6. Clarify any misunderstandings or confusion that may arise around any particular question that has been highlighted.

TEAM ASSESSMENT

Instructions: Use the scale below to indicate how each statement applies to your team. Be sure to evaluate the statements honestly and without over-thinking your answers.

3 = Usually **2 = Sometimes** **1 = Rarely**

____ 1. Team members are passionate and unguarded in their discussion of issues.

____ 2. Team members call out one another's deficiencies or unproductive behaviors.

____ 3. Team members know what their peers are working on and how they contribute to the collective good of the team.

____ 4. Team members quickly and genuinely apologize to one another when they say or do something inappropriate or possibly damaging to the team.

____ 5. Team members willingly make sacrifices (such as budget, turf, head count) in their departments or areas of expertise for the good of the team.

____ 6. Team members openly admit their weaknesses and mistakes.

____ 7. Team meetings are compelling and not boring.

____ 8. Team members leave meetings confident that their peers are completely committed to the decisions agreed upon during the meeting, even if there was initial disagreement.

____ 9. Morale is significantly affected by the failure to achieve team goals.

____10. During team meetings, the most important and most difficult issues are put on the table to be resolved.

____11. Team members are deeply concerned about the prospect of letting down their peers.

____12. Team members know about one another's personal lives and are comfortable discussing them.

____13. Team members end discussions with clear and specific resolutions and calls to action.

____14. Team members challenge one another about their plans and approaches.

____15. Team members are slow to seek credit for their own contributions but quick to point out those of others.

INDIVIDUAL SCORING

Combine your scores for the fifteen statements as indicated below.

Dysfunction 1: *Absence of Trust*	**Dysfunction 2:** *Fear of Conflict*	**Dysfunction 3:** *Lack of Commitment*	**Dysfunction 4:** *Avoidance of Accountability*	**Dysfunction 5:** *Inattention to Results*
Statement 4 ____	Statement 1 ____	Statement 3 ____	Statement 2 ____	Statement 5 ____
Statement 6 ____	Statement 7 ____	Statement 8 ____	Statement 11 ____	Statement 9 ____
Statement 12 ____	Statement 10 ____	Statement 13 ____	Statement 14 ____	Statement 15 ____
Total:	**Total:**	**Total:**	**Total:**	**Total:**

A score of 8 or 9 indicates that the dysfunction is probably not a problem for your team.

A score of 6 or 7 indicates that the dysfunction could be a problem.

A score of 3 to 5 indicates that the dysfunction needs to be addressed.

BUILDING TRUST

Personal Histories Exercise

Purpose of exercise: To improve trust by giving team members an opportunity to demonstrate vulnerability in a low-risk way, and to help team members understand one another at a fundamental level so that they can avoid making false attributions about behaviors and intentions.

Time required: Fifteen to twenty-five minutes, depending on the size of the team.

Instructions:

1. Go around the table and have everyone answer three questions about themselves, so they tell the group:

   - Where they grew up
   - How many siblings they have and where they fall in the sibling order (oldest, youngest, or whatever)
   - What was the most difficult or important challenge of their childhood

   (Note: Other questions could be used here, as long as they elicit responses calling for moderate vulnerability. For instance, "What is your favorite food?" would be bad because—in addition to being ridiculous—it would involve virtually no vulnerability. Conversely, "How do you feel about your mother?" would be bad because it would be unnecessarily personal and invasive.)

2. Ask team members what they learned about one another that they didn't know. This reinforces the purpose of the exercise and allows for a natural ending to the conversation.

BUILDING TRUST

Behavioral Profiling

Purpose of exercise: To improve trust by giving team members an opportunity to demonstrate vulnerability in an objective, in-depth way, and to help team members understand one another's strengths and weaknesses so that they can avoid making false attributions about behaviors and intentions.

Time required: Two to four hours, depending on the size of the team, the skills of the certified facilitator, and the team members' level of knowledge of the profiling tool.

Instructions: The following instructions are written with the Myers-Briggs Type Indicator (MBTI) in mind. However, the basic flow can be adapted for other tools.

1. Have all team members complete an MBTI diagnostic questionnaire at least a few days before the session begins, leaving enough time for the scores to be tabulated.
2. At the beginning of the session, present an overview of the Myers-Briggs model and the related Temperament model, giving team members an opportunity to ask questions as well as to do some qualitative assessments of their types.
3. Present team members with their MBTI scores, and help them to identify their own true type by reviewing multiple sources of data (such as indicator results, qualitative assessments, and other reading material).

4. Once all types have been identified, have team members each read a short description of their own type out loud to the rest of the team. In those instances where more than one person has the same type, have each member with that type reread the description, giving other team members an opportunity to hear the description in the context of that particular person. It is often best to stagger the reading of similar types, rather than have them read in succession, to avoid confusion and repetition.
5. List all types on a white board, and discuss with the team how the collective type of the team manifests itself. Discuss any areas where there is great consistency among the team. When there is consistency across multiple areas, identify the team type, read the one-page description of that type, and discuss its ramifications.
6. Identify potential team weaknesses or blind spots that the group must avoid as a result of its particular inclinations. Acknowledge strengths, too.
7. After the exercise has been completed, have team members read a more comprehensive description of their own type, highlighting sections that they find particularly insightful and descriptive of their tendencies. Also, have them choose one or two areas that they would like to improve about themselves, based on their Myers-Briggs type. Have all team members report these findings to the group, preferably on day two of an initial off-site.
8. Within a week of completing this exercise, have team members go back to the teams they lead and discuss their MBTI profiles. This

provides an opportunity for them to demonstrate vulnerability with their staff members, and to give them a better understanding of their probable strengths and weaknesses as a manager.

MASTERING CONFLICT

Conflict Profiling

Purpose of exercise: To identify individual and collective conflict tendencies.

Time required: Thirty to sixty minutes.

Instructions:

1. Have team members review their behavioral profile from the trust exercise, highlighting implications specific to conflict.
2. Have the team members each share those implications, along with other conflict influences in their lives, including family and life experiences as well as cultural background.
3. Discuss the similarities and differences of the team in terms of the collective outlook on conflict, as well as the potential implications.

MASTERING CONFLICT

Conflict Norming

Purpose of exercise: To provide clarity to team members about how they expect one another to engage in discussion and debate.

Time required: Thirty minutes.

Instructions:

1. Have all team members write down their individual preferences relating to acceptable and unacceptable behaviors around discussion and debate. Areas might include use of language, tone of voice, emotional content, expectations of involvement and participation, avoidance of distractions, or timeliness of response.
2. Have the members each review their preferences with the rest of the team, while someone captures key areas of similarity and difference.
3. Discuss collective preferences, paying special attention to areas of difference. Arrive at a common understanding of acceptable and unacceptable behavior that all members of the team can commit to. The leader may have to play a key role in breaking a tie.
4. Formally record and distribute behavioral expectations around conflict.

MASTERING CONFLICT

Conflict Resolution Model

Purpose of model: To help teams identify and remove extraneous obstacles that prevent them from focusing on the real issue that needs to be resolved.

Overview: The model depicted here demonstrates the different layers of obstacles that prevent teams from discussing and resolving issues. Essentially, the goal is to get to the middle of the chart, where the issue itself becomes the focus of the conversation. To get there, teams often have to acknowledge and address other topics, many of which are unrelated to the issue at hand but still create distractions and barriers.

Four different kinds of obstacles can prevent issues from being resolved:

- *Informational:* These obstacles are the easiest and most comfortable to discuss because they are actually related to the issue being discussed. To engage in the kind of conflict that achieves resolution, teams must exchange *information, facts, opinions,* and *perspectives*. This is what most teams believe they are doing, even when one of the other types of obstacles get in the way.

- *Environmental:* These are obstacles that have nothing to do with the issue being discussed, but instead involve the atmosphere in which the discussion is taking place. These might include the *physical space*. For instance, an important conversation might be

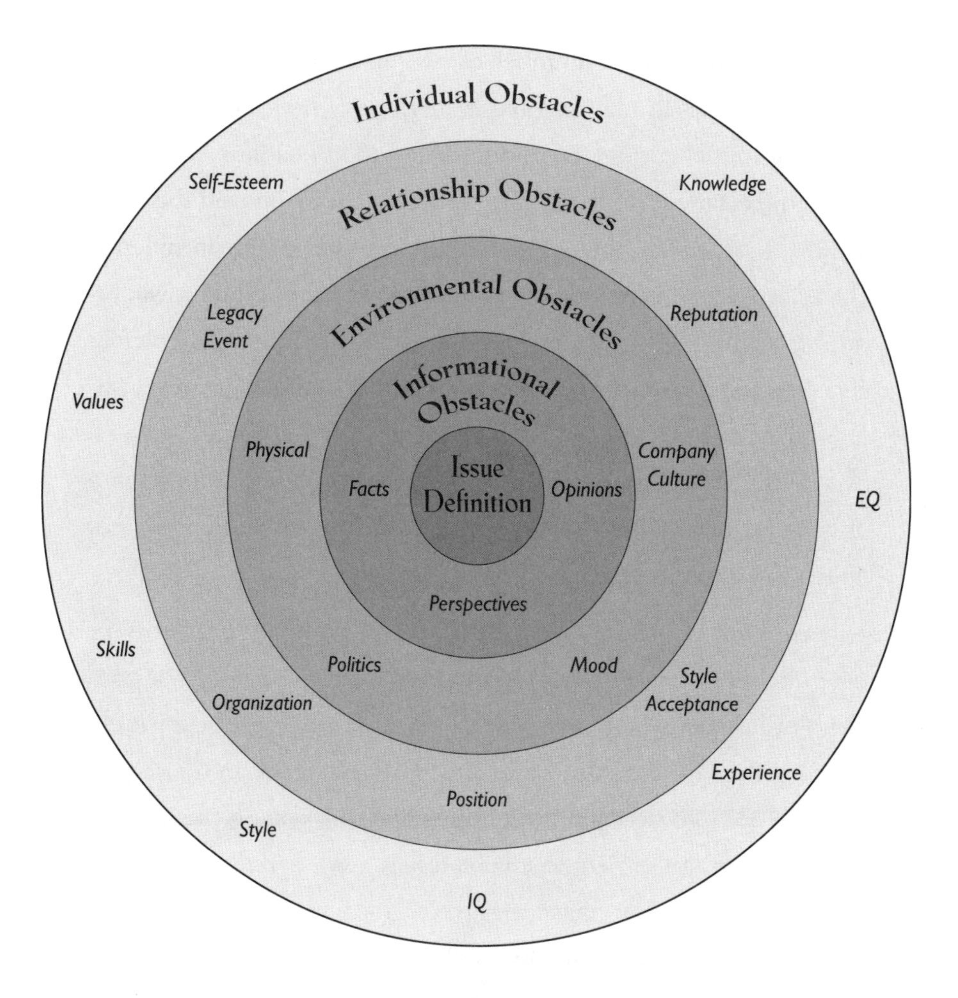

CONFLICT RESOLUTION MODEL

taking place in a hallway, in an airport, or in a conference room that is too small for the number of people attending. Or the environmental obstacle may involve *a shortage of time.* A team might be trying to make a key decision under a tight deadline, and without enough time to fully explore options. If someone on the team is in a bad *mood,* that alone can constitute an environmental obstacle because it introduces potentially distracting and misinterpreted behavior into the conversation. And certainly, *office politics* and overriding *cultural realities* within an organization can constitute environmental obstacles. A pending layoff or a war between two divisions within a company will have a profound impact on a discussion, even if the people engaged in the discussion are not directly affected by it.

- *Relationship:* These obstacles have to do with problems or issues between the very people involved in the discussion or conflict. For instance, there may have been an unresolved *legacy event* between them in the past, or such a stark difference in their *styles* that two or more people find it impossible to focus on the issue at hand. Or one of the people involved may have a *reputation,* warranted or otherwise, that negatively impacts the attitude and approach of other team members. Finally, a person's *position* in an organization or home department can color the attitudes of team members. For instance, people may be reluctant or hesitant to dive headlong into an issue with an executive two rungs above them on the organizational ladder, or team members may approach one another with bias and suspicion simply because they represent departments that have traditionally been at odds (for example, participating in the common Sales versus Marketing feud).

- *Individual:* These are obstacles that exist because one particular person involved in the discussion has a deficiency or quality that inhibits a "clean" conversation. Individual obstacles can involve insufficient *experience, IQ, knowledge, self-esteem,* or *emotional intelligence* (EQ). Or they could involve a set of *values* or *motives* that differ substantially from those of the rest of the group.

The key to using this model is to be aware of the possible existence of obstacles during discussions, and to refer to it whenever a conversation gets bogged down. Once a given obstacle is identified, a team can then either address it or, more likely, acknowledge its existence and agree not to let it color the nature of the conversation.

Obstacles on the outside of the circle are more difficult to address than those toward the middle because they involve personalities and related issues that are not changed as easily as the privacy level in a conference room or the time allotted to making a decision. Of course, the key to addressing these more challenging obstacles is trust, because the effort involves some level of personal risk.

MASTERING CONFLICT

Conflict Resolution Exercise

Purpose of exercise: To teach team members how to apply the conflict resolution model.

Time required: Thirty to sixty minutes.

Instructions:

1. As a team, choose an issue that the team has wrestled with recently—one that was (or continues to be) particularly difficult to resolve. The more difficult and complicated the issue, the better.
2. Have each member review prior discussions of the issue and analyze them according to the Conflict Resolution Model, looking for as many as possible of the different obstacles that were present during discussions.
3. Compare each team member's answers, discussing the impact that various obstacles had on the decision-making process.
4. Discuss how to address these obstacles in the future (or immediately if the example issue remains unresolved) to improve the way the team engages in conflict and makes decisions.

MASTERING CONFLICT

Depth-Frequency Conflict Model

Purpose of exercise: To help teams assess their conflict tendencies and identify areas for improvement.

Time required: Thirty minutes.

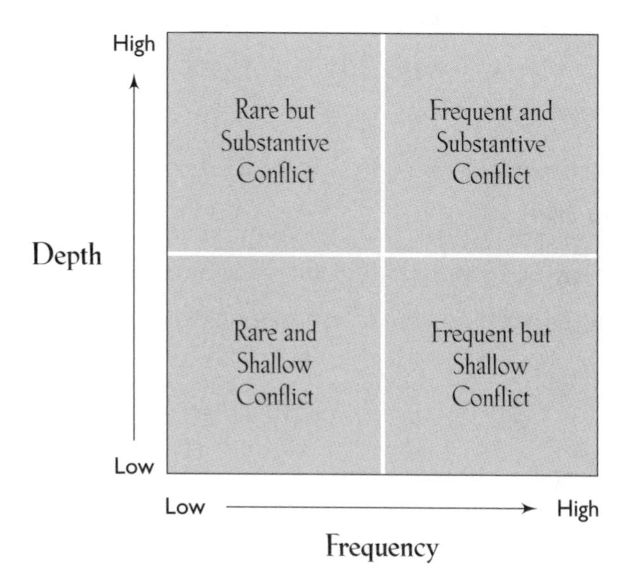

DEPTH-FREQUENCY CONFLICT MODEL

Instructions:

1. Review model with team.
2. Have the members each recreate the model on a blank sheet of paper, writing their name at the top.

3. Have them pass their sheet to the person on their left, who then places an X on the chart in the location that best indicates their perception of how the person listed at the top engages in conflict and passes the sheet along to the next member, and so on around the room.
4. When all sheets have been returned to their original owners, have team members review their own charts and indicate to the team their style according to the aggregate input of their team members.
5. Plot all team members' results on a model drawn large enough to fill a flip chart.
6. Have team members discuss the collective implications of their results, with special attention to areas of clear similarity and difference.

MASTERING CONFLICT

Thomas-Kilmann Model

Purpose of model: To help teams identify and understand their conflict tendencies and profile.

Description: The Thomas-Kilmann Model describes five different approaches to conflict according to how people think about the importance of a task versus the importance of their relationship with people they are working with. The main point of the model is to encourage people to be purposeful in how they confront and collaborate with others, rather than relying on their natural—and often inappropriate—tendencies.

For more information about this model, go to www.cpp.com.

ACHIEVING COMMITMENT

Commitment Clarification

Purpose of exercise: To ensure that teams leave meetings with no ambiguity about what they've agreed upon.

Time required: Five minutes.

Instructions:

1. Toward the end of a meeting, the leader or facilitator should go to the white board and ask the team: "What have we agreed upon today?"
2. Team members then provide their individual responses.
3. If there is no consensus, the leader then provokes further discussion to eliminate any discrepancies and clarify commitments and agreements.
4. The leader then records all commitments on the board, and has all team members record them as well.

ACHIEVING COMMITMENT

Cascading Communication

Purpose of exercise: To ensure that team members fully commit to agreements made during meetings, and to achieve alignment in the greater organization.

Time required: Five minutes.

Instructions:

1. After the Commitment Clarification Exercise has been completed, the team then decides which of the commitments and agreements should be communicated to the rest of the organization.
2. Then team members go back to the teams they lead within a given time frame (twenty-four to forty-eight hours, usually) and communicate those commitments and agreements.

Note that it is critical for cascading communication to occur either in person or live on the phone (that is, not via e-mail or voice mail) so that employees can ask questions for clarification, and so that they get a clear sense of their manager's level of commitment.

ACHIEVING COMMITMENT

Clarification of Team Principles

Purpose of exercise: To create clarity within the team around how members will deal with one another on an ongoing basis.

Time required: One or two hours.

Instructions: Have the team discuss and come to resolution around the following issues—and any others that the team deems important:

- The structure and schedule for meetings
- Acceptable behavior during meetings (for example, laptop use)
- The preferred methods for communication (for example, e-mail, voice mail, and so on) and the norms around how to use them
- The timeliness of responding to one another using those methods
- The use of common resources, human and otherwise
- The availability of team members during nonwork hours
- The level of freedom in which team members can engage one another's staffs
- The extent to which being on time is a priority

ACHIEVING COMMITMENT

Clarification of Organizational Principles

Purpose of exercise: To create clarity within the team, and the rest of the organization, around a variety of fundamental issues.

Time required: Two to five hours.

Instructions: Have the team discuss and come to resolution around some or all of the following, depending on the nature of the team and its place in the organization.

- Core purpose
- Core values
- Business definition
- Strategy
- Goals
- Roles and responsibilities

(See the book *The Four Obsessions of an Extraordinary Executive* for more details.)

ACHIEVING COMMITMENT

Establishment of Thematic Goal

Purpose of exercise: To provide the team with a common sense of purpose so that it can achieve greater alignment and avoid the emergence of silos.

Time required: Thirty to sixty minutes.

Instructions: Discuss and agree upon the thematic goal by answering the following question: *What is the single most important goal that we must achieve during this period if we are to consider ourselves successful during that time?*

The goal should not be quantitative, but rather a general achievement. Examples of common thematic goals include the following:

- Improve customer satisfaction
- Get expenses under control
- Increase market awareness
- Launch a new product
- Strengthen the team
- Rebuild the infrastructure
- Grow market share

The Challenge of Deprioritization

One of the challenges teams often face when choosing a thematic goal is best described in the questions they ask: "But don't we *always* want to be growing market share? And don't we always want to keep expenses under control?" Essentially, they're wondering if, by choosing one particular thematic goal, they're being allowed to completely ignore other areas.

Of course, the answer is no. Even when the team is focused on growing market share, it will have to keep an eye on expenses. And even when the goal is to launch a new product or establish its brand, it will have to make its numbers in terms of revenue.

However, the point of having a thematic goal is to ensure that the entire team places *extra* emphasis on a single area of priority, so that when push comes to shove, everyone understands what matters most. This helps team members avoid pulling in different directions, which leads to paralysis, frustration, and a collective silo-mentality.

The Specialist's Dilemma

Another challenge for teams trying to choose and rally around a thematic goal is this type of objection: "Hey, I'm the chief legal counsel. What do I have to do with growing market share?" Or even, "As the head of Sales, I cannot afford to take my eye off of revenue. I don't think I should be involved in getting expenses under control."

The key to overcoming this is getting everyone to understand that they must wear two different hats when they are together as a team. One of those hats, and the most important one, is that of "generic team member."

For executives, it is their "generic executive" hat. This means that they are not a functional executive, the head of a particular department. And they are not a specialist, someone who is valued because of their technical skills. They are team members who are expected to contribute to the team in any way they can. That means the head lawyer should be contributing to conversations about marketing, and that the head of Engineering should be actively involved in decisions about sales.

Now there are times when team members must put their functional hats back on so they can focus on what they must go back and accomplish within their departments. The divisions of labor that exist in any organization exist for a reason, and must be honored.

However, when team members are together, most of their focus and mind-set should be centered around collective team issues, not their own department or functional area.

Determining the Length of the Period

The time frame of the period for a thematic goal will depend on the nature of the business and industry, as well as the particular situation of the organization and team. For instance, the executive team of a start-up company will probably want to have relatively short time frames (say, two or three months), while a university might have longer cycles (for example, a year).

EMBRACING ACCOUNTABILITY

Team Effectiveness Exercise

Purpose of exercise: To give team members a forum for providing one another with focused, direct, and actionable feedback about how their individual behavior can improve the performance of the team.

Time required: One or two hours, depending on the size of the team and the skill of the facilitator.

Instructions:

1. Have all team members answer the following questions about each member of the team other than themselves:

   - What is that person's single most important behavioral quality that contributes to the strength of the team? (That is, their strength.)

   - What is that person's single most important behavioral quality that detracts from the strength of the team? (That is, their weakness or problematic behavior.)

   (Note: Team members should write down their answers so that they can commit to and remember their responses, and are not tempted to change them based on what others have said.)

2. Beginning with comments about the leader of the team, have all team members read their positive responses, one by one, until everyone has finished.

3. Ask the leader to respond to what people have said. (For example, "Any surprises? Any questions for clarification?")
4. Continuing to focus on the leader, have all team members read their negative responses, one by one, until everyone has finished.
5. Continue with this sequence for every member of the team.
6. When all team members have received input from their peers, have them each summarize aloud for the team the one or two key take-aways that they will work on individually. Have them e-mail those take-aways to the leader.
7. At the next team off-site, have the members each report on the progress they've made in regard to each of their areas for improvement. Solicit input from team members about their observations.

FOCUSING ON RESULTS

Establishment of Team Scoreboard

Purpose of tool: To provide the team with a clear and useful means of quickly assessing its success so that it can organize meetings and discussions around relevant topics.

Time required: One or two hours

Instructions: After identifying the thematic goal, have the team discuss and agree upon the handful of supporting objectives that must be accomplished if the thematic goal is to be achieved.

For instance, if the thematic goal is to focus on aggressively increasing revenue in a given period, the supporting objectives might include the following: increase marketing support, reestablish pricing and discounts, increase executive involvement in sales, expand sales efforts into new territories, hire more salespeople.

Or if the thematic goal is to increase market awareness, the supporting objectives might be to increase advertising, clarify the brand and value proposition, increase trade-show activities, and improve public relations.

All of this will depend on the unique situation of each team, as well as what is going on in the organization and the industry as a whole.

In addition to these supporting objectives, a team's scoreboard shoud include a few standard operational objectives such as revenue, expenses, employee turnover, or whatever essential metric is key to the business on an ongoing basis.

FOLLOW-UP

Initial Off-Site Follow-Up

Purpose of exercise: To ensure that progress and decisions made during the off-site are clarified, committed to, and communicated to others outside the team.

Time required: One or two hours over the course of a week.

Instructions: Immediately following the off-site, it is important for team members to follow up on particular actions to ensure the process continues to move forward. The following should happen after the meeting:

1. Team facilitator or team leader should consolidate the notes from the meeting and distribute them to the team. (This should include things like the team's personality profiles, comments from the assessment discussion, a team conflict profile, any goals and decisions that were made, and so on.)
2. Individual team members should summarize their personality profiles into three bullet points or less—things that it would be helpful for the team to keep in mind.
3. Team members need to summarize the feedback from the Team Effectiveness Exercise.
4. Team members should send their summaries to the facilitator for consolidation and distribution to the team.

GLOSSARY OF TERMS

Adrenaline addiction The unwillingness or inability of busy people to slow down and review, reflect, assess, and discuss their business and their team. An adrenaline addiction is marked by anxiety among people who always have a need to keep moving, keep spinning, even in the midst of obvious confusion and declining productivity.

Advocacy and Inquiry The two types of communication that must exist among a team. Advocacy is the statement of a belief or position. Inquiry is the active and open-minded questioning of underlying rationale or intent. These concepts were originally developed by Chris Argyris and further developed by Peter Senge.

Buy-in The achievement of honest and unwavering emotional support.

Cascading communication The activity following a meeting in which team members go to their respective departments and report on the agreed-upon decisions and outcomes. Cascading communication should take place in a timely manner following a meeting (one or two days), and occur face-to-face or live on the phone to facilitate the questions and answers.

Clarity The elimination of assumptions and ambiguity from a situation.

Collective results The idea of having goals that are shared by a team, and that transcend departments and functional areas.

Commitment The achievement of clarity and buy-in by a team around a decision, without hidden reservation or hesitation. Even when teams initially disagree about a decision, by engaging in productive conflict, they can eventually agree to a single course of action, confident that no one on the team is quietly harboring doubts.

Commitment clarification The process that takes place at the end of a meeting during which the team explicitly describes and settles on the agreements and decisions that have been made so that there is no room for ambiguity in what they subsequently do and say.

Conflict continuum The spectrum depicting the full range of conflict in an organization, from artificial harmony (zero conflict) to aggressive and destructive politics (extreme conflict). At the middle of the continuum is the point where conflict changes from constructive and ideological to destructive and personal.

Conflict norm The rules of engagement for dealing with conflict within the team. Having clear standards of behavior allows a team to focus on the discussion of issues without having to slow down to think about what is and is not appropriate.

Depth-Frequency Conflict Model A two-by-two matrix that depicts a team's conflict behavior based on the intensity and regularity with which they engage one another.

Disagree and commit The ability of team members to hold different opinions about an issue or decision and still actively support whatever final decision is made by the leader or the team as a whole.

Enter the danger The act of stepping squarely into the middle of a difficult issue. Leaders who overcome their need to avoid uncomfortable situations and enter the danger often defuse a potentially harmful issue and achieve quick resolution.

Fundamental attribution error The tendency to falsely attribute the negative behaviors of others to their character (an internal attribution), while attributing one's own negative behaviors to environmental factors (an external attribution). The fundamental attribution error often creates misunderstanding and distrust among team members. By getting to know one another better and understanding personal histories and personality tendencies, team members can often avoid this problem.

Hook A term from screenwriting, "the hook" refers to the concept of injecting drama into the first ten minutes of a meeting in order to get the attention of participants.

Initial off-site The one- or two-day kickoff of the team-building process.

Lightning round The activity at the beginning of a meeting during which team members take thirty seconds to report on their key priorities for the week.

Mining for conflict A facilitation skill that requires an individual to extract buried disagreements within a team and bring them to the surface.

Myers-Briggs Type Indicator (MBTI) A widely used personality inventory. The MBTI instrument provides a picture of people's personality type according to how they get energy, collect data, make decisions, and organize themselves.

Peer-to-peer accountability The act of team members' calling one another on behavioral or performance-related shortcomings.

Productive ideological conflict Passionate, unfiltered debate around issues that are of importance to a team. It is limited to concepts and ideas, and avoids personal attack.

Real-time permission The concept whereby a leader or facilitator interrupts a team member in the midst of healthy debate to reinforce the behavior. Real-time permission is best used when team members are not yet comfortable with conflict and need to be reminded of its importance so that they can avoid unnecessary feelings of inappropriateness.

Scoreboard A tool for displaying a team's areas of focus and evaluation of momentary success.

Self-oriented distractions Obstacles that prevent an individual from adhering to team goals because of concerns that are not necessarily relevant to the larger team. Self-oriented distractions include ego, money and career advancement, and budget and departmental needs.

Supporting objectives The components of a thematic goal, which are collectively owned by the team and often make up part of its scoreboard.

Team Effectiveness Exercise A process by which a team gives face-to-face feedback to one another, focusing on a single area of strength and a single area of weakness.

Team #1 The concept embodied by the notion that team members must prioritize the team that they are a member of over the team that they lead or manage.

Teamwork The state achieved by a group of people working together who trust one another, engage in healthy conflict, commit to decisions, hold one another accountable, and focus on collective results.

Temperament theory Temperament theory describes four personality patterns and is based in descriptions of behavior that go back over twenty-five centuries.

Thematic goal The overarching priority of a team during a given period of time. It serves as a rallying cry for the team and often helps align other parts of the organization.

Thomas-Kilmann Conflict Model A model depicting the various ways that people choose to engage in interpersonal conflict.

Vulnerability-based trust The state achieved by a team whose members are comfortable being open with one another, leaving no room for suspicion or fear of retaliation. Team members who achieve vulnerability-based trust are comfortable being exposed to one another around their failures, weaknesses, even fears.

RESOURCES

The following information is for the many of you interested in learning more about the other models and products I've referred to in this book.

MBTI®

For more information regarding the Myers-Briggs Type Indicator®, please go to www.cpp.com. CPP Inc. is the leading publisher and provider of innovative products and services for professionals focused on meeting individual and organizational development needs.

CPP Inc. and Davies-Black Publishing
3803 East Bayshore Road
P.O. Box 10096
Palo Alto, CA 94303
Phone: (650) 969-8901
Toll free: (800) 624-1765
Fax: (650) 969-8608
www.cpp.com

Thomas-Kilmann Conflict Mode Instrument

For more information regarding the Thomas-Kilmann Conflict Mode Instrument, please go to www.cpp.com. CPP Inc. is the leading publisher and provider of innovative products and services for professionals focused on meeting individual and organizational development needs.

CPP Inc. and Davies-Black Publishing
3803 East Bayshore Road
P.O. Box 10096
Palo Alto, CA 94303
Phone: (650) 969-8901
Toll free: (800) 624-1765
Fax: (650) 969-8608
www.cpp.com

Social Style Model™

For more information regarding the Social Style Model™, please go to www.tracomcorp.com. TRACOM was the original creator of the Social Style Model™, universally recognized for building interpersonal skills.

The TRACOM Group
8878 South Barrons Blvd.
Highlands Ranch, CO 80129
Phone: (303) 470-4900
Toll free: (800) 221-2321
Fax: (303) 470-4901
www.tracomcorp.com

DiSC®

For more information regarding the DiSC®, please go to www.inscapepublishing.com. Inscape pioneered the original DiSC® learning instrument over three decades ago.

Inscape Publishing
6465 Wayzata Blvd., Suite 800
Minneapolis, MN 55426
Phone: (763) 765-2222
Fax: (763) 765-2277
www.inscapepublishing.com

Insights

For more information regarding Insights, please go to www.insights.com. Insights Discovery Personal Profile is solidly based on the pioneering personality profiling work of Carl Jung.

Insights Learning & Development North America
7700 Chevy Chase Drive, Suite 1.230
Austin, TX 78752
Phone: (512) 371-9200
www.insights.com

RightPath Profiles®

For information on RightPath Resources® Profiles, please go to www.rightpath.com. RightPath Resources, Inc. provides validated online assessments to Fortune 500 companies and small businesses for use in team building, leadership development, executive coaching, hiring, and career development.

RightPath Resources, Inc.
2760 Peachtree Ind. Blvd., Suite B
Duluth, GA 30097-2201
Phone: (770) 295-1111
Toll Free: (877) THE-PATH
www.rightpath.com

TRI—Temperament Research Institute

For information on Temperament theory, please go to www.tri-network.com. TRI is a training and consulting company dedicated to serving individuals and organizations seeking to improve their overall functioning through more accurate self-knowledge, knowledge of others, effective communication, and team work.

TRI—Temperament Research Institute
P.O. Box 4457
Huntington Beach, CA 92605-4457
Toll Free: (800) 700-4874
www.tri-network.com

ACKNOWLEDGMENTS

Special thanks for this book go to the many clients who have graciously allowed my colleagues and me to come into their organizations over the years. I cannot adequately describe how much all of us at The Table Group have appreciated your passion for teamwork, your trust of our intentions, and your warmth in allowing us to become temporary members of your families.

In particular, I thank the wonderful people at VHA, Silicon Valley Bank, Alfa Insurance, The Sak, Comergent, Novell, Ritchie Capital Management, Bandag, New York Life, Veritas, Bechtel Nevada, Washington Mutual, MedPointe, Aon, Community First Credit Union, FedEx Freight, Mitsubishi, HCA Healthcare, and the many others we have worked with closely.

I also want to thank my incredible friends at The Table Group—Amy, Tracy, Michele, Karen, and Jeff—for your commitment to our clients and our own team. Working with you every day is a blessing in so many ways, and your contribution to this book was immense.

Thanks to Susan Williams, my editor, and all the folks at Jossey-Bass and Wiley, for your confidence and trust, which mean more to me with every book. And to my agent, Jim Levine, for your unquestionable commitment and passion.

As always, I thank my wife, Laura, and my boys, Connor, Matthew, and Casey, for being who you are and helping me be better than I am.

And most important, I thank God for giving me the opportunity to serve others in my small way. All glory and honor are Yours.

P.L.

ABOUT THE AUTHOR

Patrick Lencioni is founder and president of The Table Group, a management consulting firm specializing in executive team development and organizational health. As a consultant and keynote speaker, he has worked with thousands of senior executives in organizations ranging from Fortune 500s and high-tech start-ups to universities and nonprofits. Clients who have engaged his services include New York Life, Southwest Airlines, Sam's Club, Microsoft, Allstate, Visa, FedEx, and the U.S. Military Academy, West Point, to name a few. He is the author of five nationally recognized books, including the *New York Times* bestseller *The Five Dysfunctions of a Team* (Jossey-Bass, 2002).

Patrick lives in the San Francisco Bay Area with his wife, Laura, and their three sons, Matthew, Connor, and Casey.

To learn more about Patrick and The Table Group, please visit www.tablegroup.com.

To learn more about Patrick Lencioni and his other products and services, including free resources and his newsletter, please visit **www.tablegroup.com**

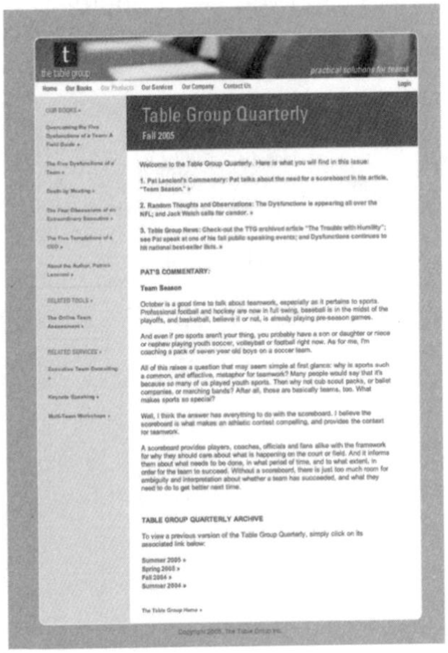

Newsletter

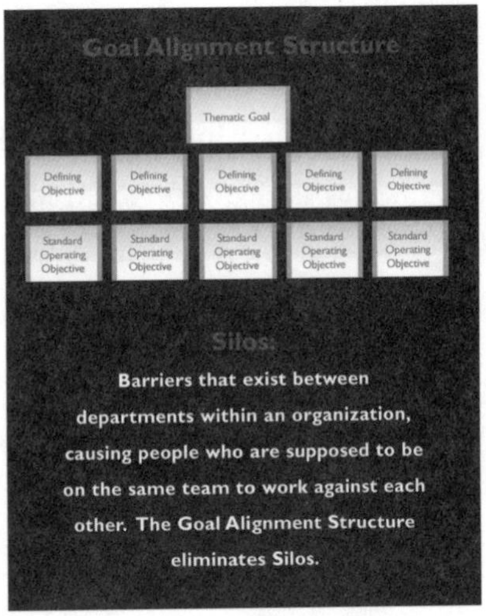

Silos Downloadable Tool

t
the table group